how2become

KS3 Maths is Easy

(Geometry & Measures)

www.How2Become.com

As part of this product you have also received FREE access to online tests that will help you to pass Key Stage 3 MATHS *(Geometry & Measures)*.

To gain access, simply go to:

www.MyEducationalTests.co.uk

Get more products for passing any test at:

www.How2Become.com

Orders: Please contact How2Become Ltd, Suite 14, 50 Churchill Square Business Centre, Kings Hill, Kent ME19 4YU.

You can order through Amazon.co.uk under ISBN: 9781911259251, via the website www.How2Become.com or through Gardners.com.

ISBN: 9781911259251

First published in 2017 by How2Become Ltd.

Typeset by How2Become Ltd.

Disclaimer

Every effort has been made to ensure that the information contained within this guide is accurate at the time of publication. How2Become Ltd is not responsible for anyone failing any part of any selection process as a result of the information contained within this guide. How2Become Ltd and their authors cannot accept any responsibility for any errors or omissions within this guide, however caused. No responsibility for loss or damage occasioned by any person acting, or refraining from action, as a result of the material in this publication can be accepted by How2Become Ltd.

The information within this guide does not represent the views of any third party service or organisation.

CONTENTS

UNDERSTANDING THE CURRICULUM

THE NATIONAL CURRICULUM

State-funded schools are governed by a set curriculum of 'core' subjects which form part of a child's education. These core subjects are essential for providing key knowledge and skills, which in turn will help us to produce well-rounded and educated citizens.

In Key Stage 3 (ages 11-14), the core subjects that must be taught in schools include the following:

- **English**
- **Maths**
- **Science**
- **Art and Design**
- **Citizenship**
- **Computing**
- **Design and Technology**
- **Languages**
- **Geography**
- **History**
- **Music**
- **Physical Education**

All schools, from Key Stage 1 to Key Stage 4, must also teach Religious Studies to their students. From the age of 11, children will also be taught Sex Education. However, parents are given the option of pulling their children out from Religious Studies and Sex Education.

THE IMPORTANCE OF MATHS

Maths is an integral subject within the national curriculum. Students should be able to understand the key concepts and different mathematical formula in order to enhance their knowledge and increase their cognitive ability.

By achieving a strong level of understanding, students are able to convey their mathematical knowledge in a range of other subjects including science, computing, and geography.

The fundamental aims of the Maths subject include:

- Using arithmetic to solve problems;

- Understanding the difference between accuracy and estimation;

- Expressing arithmetic using algebraic equations and formula;

- Learning how to carefully lay out sets of data using graphs and charts;

- Understanding averages in terms of mean, mode, median and range;

- Improving children's basic mathematical skills, before advancing on to more technical and challenging mathematical concepts;

- Improving children's confidence in their mathematical abilities, allowing them to grasp different topics of maths and how they can apply these techniques to their work.

In Key Stage 3, maths is broken down into several modules:

- **Numbers and Calculations;**

- **Ratio, Proportion and Rates of Change;**

- **Geometry and Measures;**

- **Working with Algebra;**

- **Probability and Statistics.**

The aforementioned modules are all used to teach students the vital skills for both academia and the outside world.

Pupils will be able to recognise different mathematic concepts and apply them to different calculations. In Key Stage 3, it is important that students are able to move fluently through the subject, and demonstrate a wide range of skills.

Key Stage 3 is a crucial time in academic terms, as it prepares students for their GCSEs. Every pupil will be required to take Maths as a GCSE, and therefore having a strong knowledge in these starter years at secondary school, will put students in the position that they are expected to be in before entering their GCSEs.

MATHS SUBJECT CONTENT

Below we have broken down the aims and objectives of each 'module' for Maths. This will hopefully give you some idea of what will be assessed, and how you can improve different areas in the mathematics subject.

PROBABILITY AND STATISTICS

<u>Pupils will be taught how to:</u>

☐ Understand the probability of an outcome.

☐ Record, describe and analyse the frequency of outcomes of simple probability experiments involving randomness, fairness, equally and unequally outcomes, using mathematical language, and the use of a probability scale from 0-1.

☐ Enumerate data and understand information provided in the form of:

Tables, grids, graphs and charts, Venn diagrams and pictograms.

☐ Describe, interpret and compare information from graphical representations.

☐ Understand the mean, mode, median and range of a set of data, and comparing this to other similar data.

☐ Construct graphs and charts in order to represent a set of data. Pupils should understand what type of graph or chart works best for the data they have collated.

NUMBERS AND CALCULATIONS

Pupils will be taught how to:

☐ Apply the concepts of the following mathematical numbers:

Prime numbers, factors, multiples, common factors, common multiples, highest common factor (HCF), lowest common multiple (LCM) and prime factorisation

☐ Use place values for working out decimals, measures and integers of any size

☐ Order numbers in terms of positive and negative. Students should also have a strong grasp of mathematical symbols including:

=, ≠, ≤, ≥

☐ Use brackets, powers, roots and reciprocals.

☐ Use different standard units of measure including:

Mass, length, time and money.

☐ Round numbers up and down to the correct degree of accuracy. Students will be taught about significant figures and decimal places.

☐ Correctly use a calculator, and learn all of the key buttons on a scientific calculator.

☐ Interpret percentages as being 'a number out of 100'. Pupils will also be taught how to use percentages higher than 100%, how to convert a percentage into a fraction or decimal, and how to find the percentage of a number.

☐ Recognise square and cube numbers, and understanding the importance of powers 2, 3, 4 and 5.

☐ Appreciate the infinite nature of the sets of integers, real and rational numbers.

☐ Interpret and compare numbers in standard form $A \times 10^N$ $1 \leq A < 10$, where N is a positive or negative integer or zero.

RATIO, PROPORTION AND RATES OF CHANGE

<u>Pupils will be taught how to:</u>

☐ Change between different standard units. For example:

Length, area, time volume and mass.

☐ Use ratio notation, including reduction to simplest form.

☐ Use scale factors, scale diagrams and maps.

☐ Express one quantity as a fraction of another, where the fraction is less than 1 and greater than 1.

☐ Divide a given quantity into two parts in given part:part or part:whole ratio; express the division of a quantity into two parts as a ratio.

☐ Understand that a multiplicative relationship between two quantities can be expressed as a ratio or a fraction.

☐ Relate the language of ratios and the associated calculations to the arithmetic of fractions and to linear functions.

☐ Solve problems involving percentage change including:

Percentage increase, percentage decrease, original value problems and simple interest in financial mathematics

☐ Solve problems involving direct and inverse proportion, including graphical and algebraic representations.

☐ Using compound units such as speed, unit pricing and density to solve problems.

WORKING WITH ALGEBRA

Pupils will be taught how to:

☐ Use and interpret algebraic notations, including:

ab in place of a x b;

3y in place of y + y + y and 3 x y;

a^2 in place of a x a, a3 in place of a x a x a, a^2b in place of a x a x b;

$a/_b$ in place of a ÷ b;

Coefficients written as fractions rather than as decimals;

Brackets.

☐ Substitute numerical values into formulae and expressions, including scientific formulae.

☐ Understand and use the concepts and vocabulary of expressions, equations, inequalities, terms and factors.

☐ Simplify and manipulate algebraic expressions to maintain equivalence by:

Collecting like terms;

Multiplying a single term over a bracket;

Taking out common factors;

Expanding products of two or more binomials.

☐ Recognise, sketch and produce graphs of linear and quadratic functions of one variable with appropriate scaling, using equations in x and y and the Cartesian plane.

☐ Use linear and quadratic graphs to estimate values of y for given values of x and vice versa and to find approximate solutions of simultaneous linear equations.

☐ Recognise arithmetic sequences and find the nth term.

☐ Find approximate solutions to contextual problems from given graphs of a variety of functions, including piece-wise linear, exponential and reciprocal graphs.

☐ Reduce a given linear equation in two variables to the standard form $y = mx + c$; calculate and interpret gradients and intercepts of graphs of such linear equations numerically, graphically and algebraically.

☐ Recognise geometric sequences and appreciate other sequences that arise.

GEOMETRY AND MEASURES

Pupils will be taught how to:

☐ Derive and apply formulae to calculate and solve problems including:

Perimeter and area of triangles, parallelograms, trapezia, volume of cuboids (including cubes) and other prisms (including cylinders).

☐ Calculate and solve problems involving: perimeters of 2-D shapes (including circles), areas of circles and composite shapes.

☐ Draw and measure line segments and angles in geometric figures, including interpreting scale drawings.

☐ Derive and use the standard ruler and compass constructions (perpendicular bisector of a line segment, constructing a perpendicular to a given line from/at a given point, bisecting a given angle); recognise and use the perpendicular distance from a point to a line as the shortest distance to the line.

☐ Describe, sketch and draw using conventional terms and notations:

Points, lines, parallel lines, perpendicular lines, right angles, regular polygons, and other polygons that are reflectively and rotationally symmetric.

☐ Use the standard convention for labelling the sides and angles of triangle ABC, and know and use the criteria for congruence of triangles.

☐ Derive and illustrate properties of triangles, quadrilaterals, circles and other place figures [for example, equal lengths and angles] using appropriate language and technologies.

☐ Use Pythagoras' Theorem and trigonometric ratios in similar triangles to solve problems involving right-angled triangles.

☐ Use properties of faces, surfaces, edges and vertices of cubes, cuboids, prisms, cylinders, pyramids, cones and spheres to solve problems in 3-D.

☐ Interpret mathematical relationships both algebraically and geometrically.

☐ Identify properties of, and describe the results of, translations, rotations and reflections applied to given figures.

☐ Identify and construct triangles, and construct congruent triangles, and construct similar shapes by enlargements, with and without coordinate grids.

☐ Apply the properties of angles at a point, angles at a point on a straight line, vertically opposite angles.

☐ Understand and use the relationship between parallel lines and alternate and corresponding angles.

Maths is not only a core subject in schools, but is also a topic that impacts upon every aspect of our daily lives. As you can see, it is imperative that students are able to engage in mathematics, in order to improve on vital skills and knowledge.

USING THIS GUIDE

This guide focuses specifically on Key Stage 3 Maths (Geometry & Measures). This book will cover everything you will need to know in terms of different shapes and measurements.

REMEMBER – It's really important that you have a good mathematical understanding, as this will help you through other school subjects, and in day-to-day activities.

HOW WILL I BE ASSESSED?

At Key Stage 3, children will be assessed based on Levels. These years do not count towards anything, and are simply a reflection of progression and development. The first years of secondary school are in place in order to determine whether or not pupils are meeting the minimum requirements, and are therefore an integral stage for preparing pupils for their GCSE courses.

Although these years do not count towards any final results, they do go a long way in deciphering which GCSEs you will pick up. For example, if you were excelling in Maths at KS3, you could consider taking this subject at A Level, and even Higher Education!

The subjects that you choose at GCSE will impact upon your future aspirations, including further education and career opportunities.

You will be monitored and assessed throughout these schooling years, via the following:

- Ongoing teacher assessments;

- Term progress reports;

- Summative assessments at the end of each academic year.

By the end of Key Stage 3, pupils are expected to achieve Levels 5 or 6.

INCREASE YOUR CHANCES

Below is a list of GOLDEN NUGGETS that will help YOU and your CHILD to prepare for Key Stage 3 Maths.

Golden Nugget 1 – Revision timetables

When it comes to revising, preparation is key. That is why you need to sit down with your child and come up with an efficient and well-structured revision timetable.

It is important that you work with your child to assess their academic strengths and weaknesses, in order to carry out these revision sessions successfully.

TIP – Focus on their weaker areas first!

TIP – Create a weekly revision timetable to work through different subject areas.

TIP – Spend time revising with your child. Your child will benefit from your help and this is a great way for you to monitor their progress.

Golden Nugget 2 – Understanding the best way your child learns

There are many different ways to revise when it comes to exams, and it all comes down to picking a way that your child will find most useful.

Below is a list of the common learning styles that you may want to try with your child:

- **Visual** – the use of pictures and images to remember information.

- **Aural** – the use of sound and music to remember information.

- **Verbal** – the use of words, in both speech and writing, to understand information.

- **Social** – working together in groups.

- **Solitary** – working and studying alone.

Popular revision techniques include: *mind mapping, flash cards, making notes, drawing flow charts,* and *diagrams.* You could instruct your child on how to turn diagrams and pictures into words, and words into diagrams. Try as many different methods as possible, to see which style your child learns from the most.

TIP – Work out what kind of learner your child is. What method will they benefit from the most?

TIP – Try a couple of different learning aids and see if you notice a change in your child's ability to understand what is being taught.

Golden Nugget 3 – Break times

Allow your child plenty of breaks when revising.

It's really important not to overwork your child.

TIP – Practising for 10 to 15 minutes per day will improve your child's reading ability.

TIP – Keep in mind that a child's retention rate is usually between 30 to 50 minutes. Any longer than this, and your child will start to lose interest.

Golden Nugget 4 – Practice, practice and more practice!

Purchase past practice papers. This is a fantastic way for you to gain an idea of how your child is likely to be tested.

Golden Nugget 5 – Understanding different areas in Maths

As with any subject, Maths has a range of different modules. Therefore, your child may find one module easier than another. We recommend that you spend time focusing on one module at a time. This will ensure that your child knows everything they should about each module – before moving on to the next.

TIP – Know what modules you need to focus on!

Golden Nugget 6 – Improve their confidence

Encourage your child to interact with you, their peers and their teachers. If they are struggling, they need to be able to reach out and ask for help. By asking for help, they will be able to work on their weaknesses, and therefore increase their overall performance and confidence.

TIP – Talk to your child and work through different Maths questions with them.

Golden Nugget 7 – Stay positive!

The most important piece of preparation advice we can give you, is to make sure that your child is positive and relaxed about these tests.

Don't let assessments worry you, and certainly don't let them worry your child.

TIP – Make sure the home environment is as comfortable and relaxed as possible for your child.

Golden Nugget 8 – Answer the easier questions first

A good tip to teach your child is to answer all the questions they find easiest first. That way, they can swiftly work through the paper, before attempting the questions they struggle with.

TIP – Get your child to undergo a practice paper. Tell them to fill in the answers that they find the easiest first. That way, you can spend time helping your child with the questions they find more difficult.

Spend some time working through the questions they find difficult and make sure that they know how to work out the answer.

Golden Nugget 9 – Understanding mathematical terminology

The next section is a glossary containing all the mathematical terminology that your child should familiarise themselves with.

Sit down with your child and learn as many of these KEY TERMS as you can.

> *TIP – Why not make your child's learning fun? Write down all of the terms and cut them out individually. Do the same for the definitions.*
>
> *Get your child to try and match the KEY TERM with its definition. Keep playing this game until they get them all right!*

Golden Nugget 10 – Check out our other revision resources

We have a range of other KS3 Maths resources to help your child prepare for EVERY stage of their mathematical learning.

LEARN YOUR

MATHS

TERMINOLOGY

ACUTE ANGLES	An angle less than 90˚.
ALGEBRA	The part of maths where symbols and letters are used to represent numbers.
AREA	A measurement of a surface. For the area of a square, you would multiply the height by the width.
BIDMAS	**B**rackets, **I**ndices, **D**ivision, **M**ultiplication, **A**ddition, **S**ubtraction.
CIRCUMFERENCE	The distance around something. It is the enclosing boundary of a curved geometric figure.
COMPOUND SHAPE	A compound shape includes two or more simple shapes.
CUBED NUMBERS	A cubed number is a number multiplied by itself, three times.
DECIMAL PLACES	The position of a digit to the right of a decimal point.
DECIMAL	A type of number, for example 0.5 is equivalent to 50%.
DIAMETER	A straight line passing side-to-side through the middle of a circle.
EQUILATERAL TRIANGLE	A type of triangle. All sides and angles are of equal value. All angles are 60˚.
ESTIMATION	A rough calculation or guess.
FACTOR	A factor is a number that can be divided wholly into another number. For example, 4 is a factor of 8.
FRACTIONS	A type of number, for example ½ is equivalent to a half.
FREQUENCY	The frequency of a specific data is the number of times that number occurs. (Frequent).
HIGHEST COMMON FACTOR (HCF)	To find the HCF, you need to find all of the factors of two or more numbers, and then see which number is the highest.

IMPERIAL UNITS	Imperial units of length, mass and capacity. Includes inch, foot, yard, ounce, pound, stone, pint and gallon.
ISOSCELES TRIANGLE	A type of triangle. Two sides and angles are of the same value.
LOWEST COMMON MULTIPLE (LCM)	To find the LCM, you need to find all of the multiples of two or more numbers, and then work out the lowest number in common.
MEAN	A type of average. Add up all of the numbers and divide it by how many numbers there are.
MEDIAN	A type of average. Rearrange the numbers in ascending order. What number is in the middle?
METRIC UNITS	Metric units of length, mass and capacity. Includes mm, cm, km, mg, g, kg, ml and litres.
MODE	A type of average. What number occurs the most?
MULTIPLE	A multiple simply means 'times tables'. The multiples of 2 are 2, 4, 6, 8 and so on.
NEGATIVE NUMBER	A negative number is a number less than 0. On a scale, positive numbers move to the right, and negative numbers move to the left. Indicated by the sign '-'. For example, -4.
OBTUSE ANGLE	A type of angle. An obtuse angle is more than $90°$ but less than $180°$.
PARALLEL LINE	A parallel line is two or more lines that are always the same distance apart, and never touch.
PERIMETER	A measurement of a surface. The line forming the boundary of a closed geometrical figure.
PERPENDICULAR LINES	A perpendicular line is two lines that meet at a right angle ($90°$).
PI	The mathematic constant 3.14159... The ratio of a circle's circumference to its diameter.

POSITIVE NUMBER	A positive number is a number more than 0. On a scale, positive numbers move to the right, and negative numbers move to the left.
PROBABILITY	The extent to whether something is likely to occur.
RADIUS	The radius is a straight line.
RANGE	A type of average. The range between the largest number and the smallest number.
RATIO	The quantitative relation between two amounts showing the number of times one value contain or is contained within the other.
REFLEX ANGLE	A type of angle. A reflex angle is more than 180° but less than 360°.
RIGHT-ANGLED TRIANGLE	A type of triangle. A triangle that has a 90° angle.
SCALENE TRIANGLE	A triangle with no equal angles or equal length sides.
SIGNIFICANT FIGURES	The digits carrying meaning. This allows us get a rough idea. For example, 48,739. The '4' is a significant figure because it represents 40 thousand.
SIMPLIFYING FRACTIONS	A way of making a fraction easier to read by finding a whole number that can be divided equally into both the denominator and numerator. For example, 12/24 can be simplified to 1/2. Both '12' and '24' can be divided by 12.
SQUARED NUMBER	A square number is the number that is reached when multiplying two of the same numbers together. For example 9 is the square number of 3 x 3.
SYMMETRY	Symmetry is when one shape becomes exactly like another if it's flipped or rotated.
VOLUME	The amount of space that a shape or object occupies. Contained within a container.

REGULAR AND IRREGULAR POLYGONS
POLYGONS
(TYPES OF SHAPES)

REGULAR POLYGONS

A regular polygon is a shape which has sides of equal lengths. All of its interior angles are of equal size.

Check out our YouTube channel

CAREERVIDZ

for more information on polygons and 2D shapes.

Let's go through some of the properties of some regular polygon shapes.

TRIANGLE	NO. OF SIDES	LINES OF SYMMETRY	ROTATIONAL SYMMETRY
	• 3 sides	• 3 lines of symmetry	• Rotational symmetry of order 3

QUADRILATERAL	NO. OF SIDES	LINES OF SYMMETRY	ROTATIONAL SYMMETRY
	• 4 sides	• 4 lines of symmetry	• Rotational symmetry of order 4

PENTAGON	NO. OF SIDES	LINES OF SYMMETRY	ROTATIONAL SYMMETRY
	• 5 sides	• 5 lines of symmetry	• Rotational symmetry of order 5

HEXAGON	NO. OF SIDES	LINES OF SYMMETRY	ROTATIONAL SYMMETRY
	• 6 sides	• 6 lines of symmetry	• Rotational symmetry of order 6

HEPTAGON	NO. OF SIDES	LINES OF SYMMETRY	ROTATIONAL SYMMETRY
	• 7 sides	• 7 lines of symmetry	• Rotational symmetry of order 7

OCTAGON	NO. OF SIDES	LINES OF SYMMETRY	ROTATIONAL SYMMETRY
	• 8 sides	• 8 lines of symmetry	• Rotational symmetry of order 8

IRREGULAR POLYGONS

An irregular polygon is a shape which has different size lengths. All of its interior angles are of different size.

Let's go through some of the properties of some irregular polygon shapes.

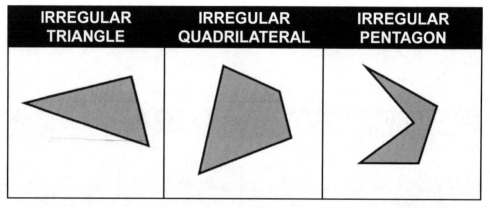

IRREGULAR TRIANGLE	IRREGULAR QUADRILATERAL	IRREGULAR PENTAGON

- The triangle has 3 different side lengths. Its angles would also be different.

- The quadrilateral has 4 different side lengths. Its angles would also be different.

- The pentagon has 5 different side lengths. Its angles would also be different.

IRREGULAR HEXAGON	IRREGULAR HEPTAGON	IRREGULAR OCTAGON

- The hexagon has 6 different side lengths. Its angles would also be different.

- The heptagon has 7 different side lengths. Its angles would also be different.

- The octagon has 8 different side lengths. Its angles would also be different.

Have a go at drawing your own irregular polygons. Remember, that the shape can look as wacky as you like!

Question Time!

QUESTION 1

What is a regular polygon?

_____

_____

_____

QUESTION 2

What is an irregular polygon?

_____

_____

_____

QUESTION 3

Fill in the table about shapes and sides.

Name of shape	No. of sides	Lines of symmetry
Square		
	6	
		8
Heptagon		

QUESTION 4

For each of the shapes below, write whether that shape is a **regular** or **irregular** polygon.

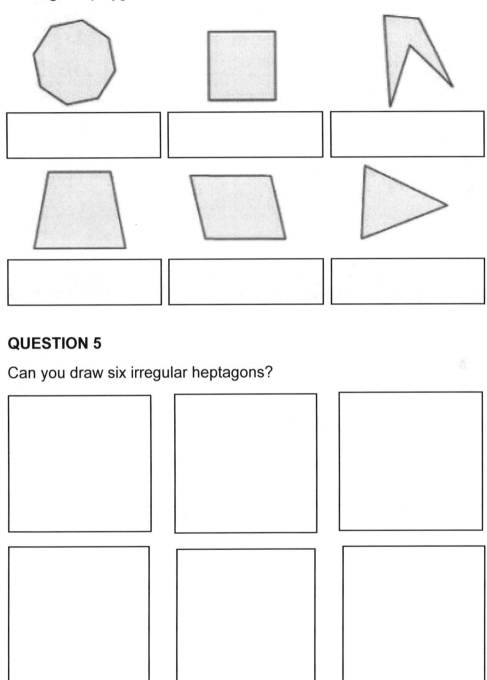

QUESTION 5

Can you draw six irregular heptagons?

Answers

Q1.

A regular polygon is a shape which contains sides of equal lengths. All of its interior angles are of equal size.

Q2.

An irregular polygon is a shape which contains sides of different lengths. All of its interior angles are of different size.

Q3.

Name of shape	No. of sides	Lines of symmetry
Square	4	4
Hexagon	6	6
Octagon	8	8
Heptagon	7	7

Q4.

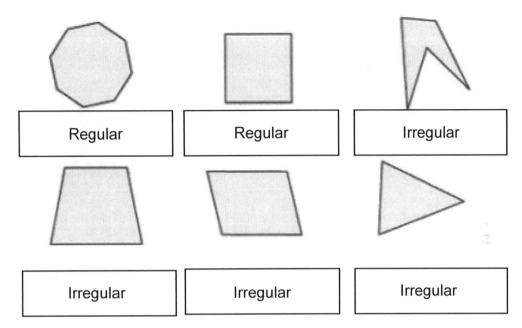

Regular	Regular	Irregular
Irregular	Irregular	Irregular

Q5.

You could have drawn any shape as long as it contained 7 sides of different lengths, and angles of different sizes.

<u>For example:</u>

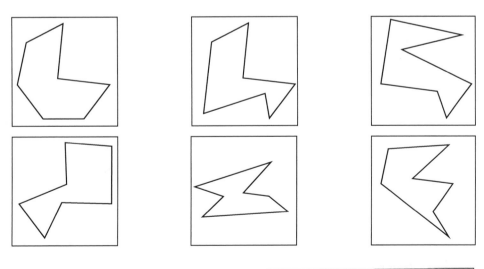

TRIANGLES
(TYPES OF SHAPES)

TRIANGLES

There are four different types of triangles that you will need to learn.

EQUILATERAL TRIANGLE	SIDES	ANGLES	SYMMETRY
	• 3 **equal** sides	• 3 **equal** angles of 60°	• 3 lines of symmetry • Rotational symmetry of order 3

ISOSCELES TRIANGLE	SIDES	ANGLES	SYMMETRY
	• 2 **equal** sides	• 2 angles of the same size	• 1 line of symmetry • No rotational symmetry

NOTE: the dashed lines on the sides of the isosceles triangle indicates that the two sides are of the same length.

There would be dashed lines on all sides of the equilateral triangle, but the dotted symmetry line is hiding them!

SCALENE TRIANGLE	SIDES	ANGLES	SYMMETRY
	• All sides are different	• All angle sizes are different	• No line of symmetry • No rotational symmetry

RIGHT-ANGLED TRIANGLE	SIDES	ANGLES	SYMMETRY
90°	• All sides are different	• 1 right angle (90˚)	• No line of symmetry • No rotational symmetry

BASIC MATHS

Types of triangles

Check out our Youtube channel

CAREERVIDZ

for more information on types of triangles.

Question Time!

QUESTION 1

For each of the triangles, write whether the triangle is an **equilateral, isosceles, scalene** or **right-angled**.

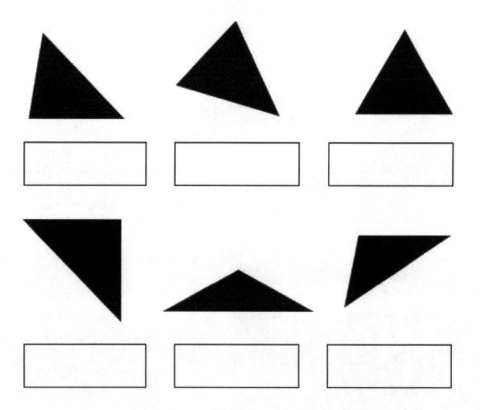

QUESTION 2

Complete the table about the properties of triangles.

TRIANGLE	SIDES	ANGLES	LINES OF SYMMETRY
	2 side lengths of the same size		
			3 lines of symmetry
Scalene			

QUESTION 3

Which of the 5 triangles below would you need to use in order to make a square?

The triangles will not need to be rotated or reflected, nor do their sizes change.

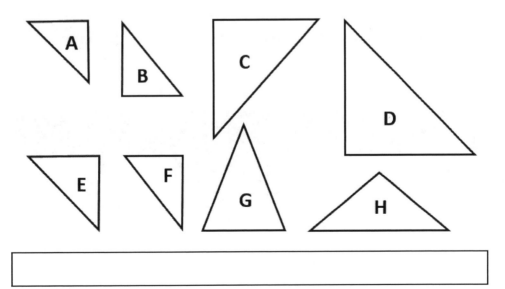

Answers

Q1.

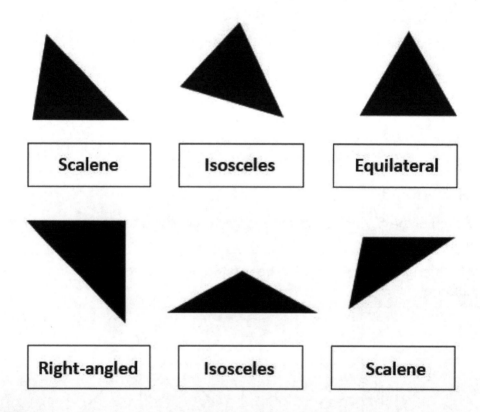

| Scalene | Isosceles | Equilateral |

| Right-angled | Isosceles | Scalene |

Q2.

Isosceles	2 side lengths of the same size	2 angles of the same size	1 line of symmetry
Equilateral	3 side lengths of equal size	3 angles of 60°	3 lines of symmetry
Scalene	No side lengths the same size	No angles the same size	No line of symmetry

Q3.

A, B, D, E and F = when positioned together, all of these triangles make a square.

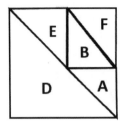

QUADRILATERALS
(TYPES OF SHAPES)

QUADRILATERALS

The word 'quadrilateral' refers to a 4-sided shape.

QUAD = FOUR

SQUARE	SIDES	ANGLES	SYMMETRY
	• 4 **equal** sides	• 4 **equal** angles of 90°	• 4 lines of symmetry • Rotational symmetry of order 4

RECTANGLE	SIDES	ANGLES	SYMMETRY
	• 2 **pairs** of **equal** sides (opposite sides are equal)	• 4 **equal** angles of 90°	• 2 lines of symmetry • Rotational symmetry of order 2

RHOMBUS / DIAMOND (pushed over square)	SIDES	ANGLES	SYMMETRY
	• 4 **equal** sides (opposite sides are parallel)	• 2 **pairs** of **equal** angles	• 2 lines of symmetry • Rotational symmetry of order 2

PARALLELOGRAM (pushed over rectangle)	SIDES	ANGLES	SYMMETRY
	• 2 **pairs** of **equal** sides (opposite sides are parallel)	• 2 **pairs** of **equal** angles	• No lines of symmetry • Rotational symmetry of order 2

TRAPEZIUM	SIDES	ANGLES	SYMMETRY
	• 1 **pair** of parallel sides	• Vary depending on the trapezium	• No lines of symmetry (except an isosceles trapezium) • No rotational symmetry

KITE	SIDES	ANGLES	SYMMETRY
	• 2 **pairs** of **equal** sides (opposite sides are parallel)	• 2 **pairs** of **equal** angles	• 1 line of symmetry • No rotational symmetry

BASIC MATHS Learning Your 2D Shapes

Check out our Youtube channel

CAREERVIDZ

for more information on quadrilaterals and other 2D shapes.

Question Time!

QUESTION 1

Match up the descriptions to the correct quadrilateral.

1 pair of equal angles. 2 pairs of equal sides. No rotational symmetry.	SQUARE
2 lines of symmetry. 4 equal angles of 90°.	RECTANGLE
4 lines of symmetry. 4 equal angles of 90°.	KITE

QUESTION 2

For the above question, using a ruler, a protractor and a pen, draw these three quadrilaterals.

Things to consider:

- Drawing the correct angles;
- Drawing straight lines;
- Labelling the angles;
- Adding in dashes on lines that are parallel.

QUESTION 3

Below is a flow chart classifying the different types of quadrilaterals.
Write which quadrilateral it is describing in the boxes below.

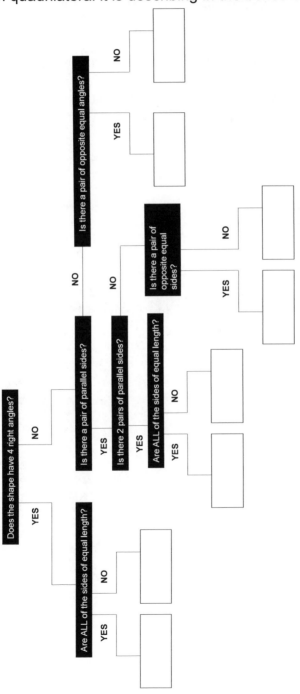

QUESTION 4

For the following statements, circle whether they are **true** or **false**.

A quadrilateral will always have one angle less than or equal to 90°.

TRUE / FALSE

A square is the only quadrilateral to have four 90° angles.

TRUE / FALSE

A trapezium has no rotational symmetry.

TRUE / FALSE

A parallelogram is a square pushed over.

TRUE / FALSE

QUESTION 5

Complete the word search below.

```
W E F P W H Z E Z M B L A B E K F F F U       PARALLELOGRAM
E P A T X R N S P A X G K U I Y B W Z W       TRAPEZIUM
L C Y X D F E D W R I K A T L A V S S J       KITE
G Q N Y V G R X N G Y L E Y U P P E U H       RHOMBUS
N J D F V C A C W O L D T F T E D H B Y       SQUARE
A N A S X D U H F L M D D J C I C P M K       RECTANGLE
T M F W L K Q H D E R A V V S Q A O O L       DIAMOND
C B W U T A S U V L S Y I B P D D E H R       PARALLEL
E X E V P O R I E L M O B D D Z W T R A       SYMMETRY
R S W E M R L E P A Z H Y R M Q O K Y B       ANGLES
A B Q W K K D P T R U V M J R Y A K W R       SIDES
M U I Z E P A R T A A J V F R Y A I U T       FOUR
Q C N H O R S L G P L I G T U Q K O Y T       QUADRILATERALS
T S J I A A O J E I W I E H S W F X U O
Y D P L S G T Q T A O M R T M H A B O F
H W L Y G R H K U N M H D D J Q G V D Q
T E E P K H G A K Y B M H L A M I C S K
L A N G L E S G S E M T J X K U V O Q F
Z N H N V N F O F P N Y G C F R Q V L Y
A Y E S D S G W H W I A T V V K L S L Z
```

Answers

Q1.

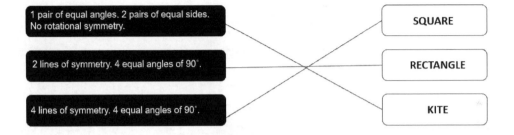

1 pair of equal angles. 2 pairs of equal sides. No rotational symmetry.	SQUARE
2 lines of symmetry. 4 equal angles of 90°.	RECTANGLE
4 lines of symmetry. 4 equal angles of 90°.	KITE

Q2.

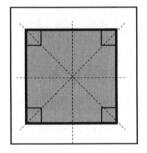
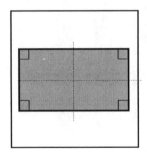
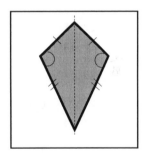

Q3.

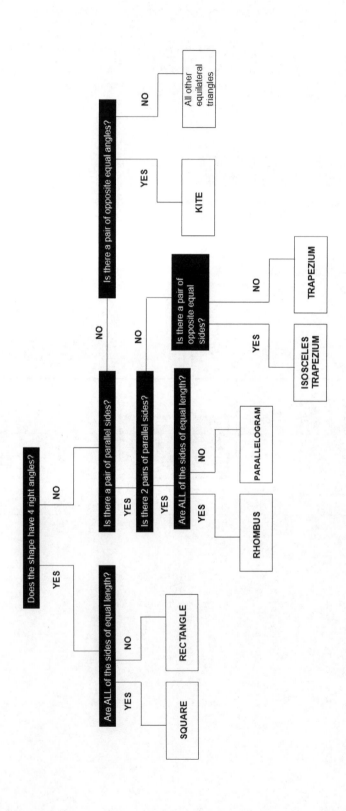

Q4.

A quadrilateral will always have one angle less than or equal to 90˚.

TRUE

A square is the only quadrilateral to have four 90˚ angles.

FALSE

A trapezium has no rotational symmetry.

TRUE

A parallelogram is a square pushed over.

FALSE

Q5.

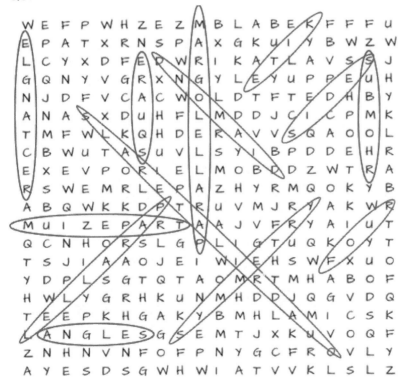

HOW ARE YOU GETTING ON?

CIRCLES

(TYPES OF SHAPES)

CIRCLES

When it comes to circles, there are a lot of tricky words to get your head around!

RADIUS, DIAMETER AND CIRCUMFERENCE

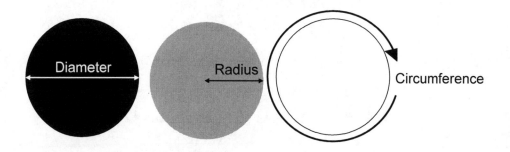

DIAMETER

The distance running right through the centre of the circle, from one side of the circle, to the other.

RADIUS

The radius is half the length of the diameter.

Starting from the middle of the circle, the radius reaches the edge of the circle.

CIRCUMFERENCE

The circumference is the outer edge of a circle.

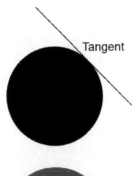

TANGENT

A tangent is a straight line which touches the outer side of the circle.

CHORD

A chord is a straight line drawn across the inside of a circle, but DOES NOT run through the centre.

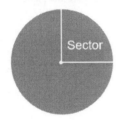

SECTOR

A sector is like a 'piece' or 'slice'. Using the mid-point of the circle, create two straight lines which reach the edge of the circle.

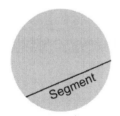

SEGMENT

A segment is the area you get when you draw a chord. The chord is the line, whereas the segment is the area in that chord.

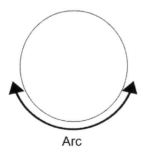

Arc

ARC

An arc is part of the circumference of the circle.

Question Time!

QUESTION 1

Match the circle terms with the correct description.

The area you get when you cut through a circle with a chord.	TANGENT
The outer edge of a circle.	RADIUS
Part of the circumference.	ARC
The mid-point of a circle to the edge of a circle.	CIRCUMFERENCE
A straight line which touches the outside of a circle.	SEGMENT
A 'piece' of the circle (i.e. a wedged-shape area).	DIAMETER
A straight line which goes straight through the circle, passing through the mid-point.	SECTOR

QUESTION 2

For each of the following statements, circle whether it is **true** or **false**.

If the radius of a circle is 8cm, then the diameter of the circle will be 4cm.

TRUE / FALSE

A chord is similar to a diameter in that it's drawn from one side of the circle to the other.

TRUE / FALSE

The radius is half the length of the diameter.

TRUE / FALSE

QUESTION 3

On the circle images below, draw the following:

a) An arc

b) The circumference

c) A segment

d) A sector

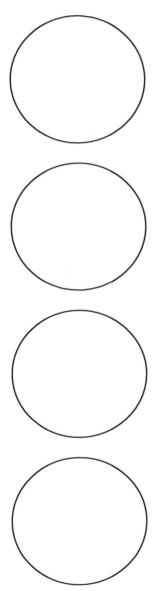

Answers

Q1.

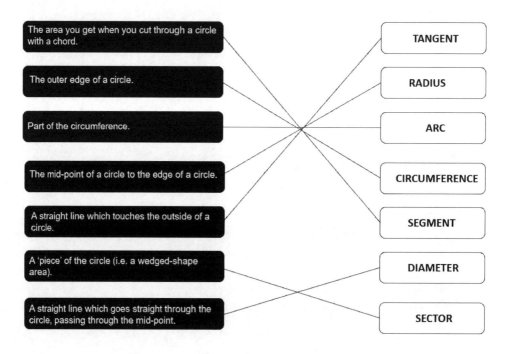

The area you get when you cut through a circle with a chord.	TANGENT
The outer edge of a circle.	RADIUS
Part of the circumference.	ARC
The mid-point of a circle to the edge of a circle.	CIRCUMFERENCE
A straight line which touches the outside of a circle.	SEGMENT
A 'piece' of the circle (i.e. a wedged-shape area).	DIAMETER
A straight line which goes straight through the circle, passing through the mid-point.	SECTOR

Q2.

If the radius of a circle is 8cm, then the diameter of the circle will be 4cm.

FALSE

A chord is similar to a diameter in that it's drawn from one side of the circle to the other.

TRUE

The radius is half the length of the diameter.

TRUE

Q3.

a)

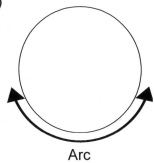

Arc

b)

Circumference

c)

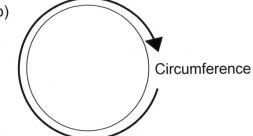

Segment

d)

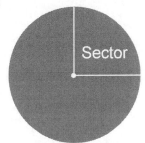

Sector

3D SHAPES

(TYPES OF SHAPES)

3D SHAPES

3D shapes are SOLID shapes.

Check out our YouTube channel

CAREERVIDZ

for more information on 3D shapes.

There are eight 3D shapes you need to know off by heart!

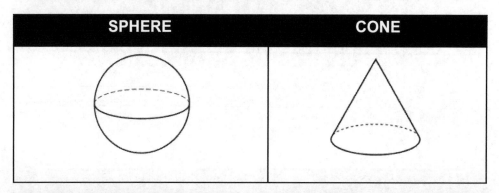

| SPHERE | CONE |

| CUBE | CUBOID |

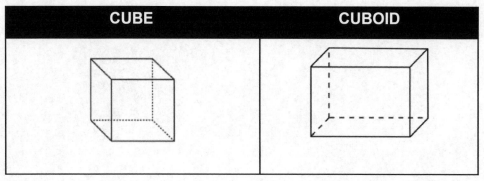

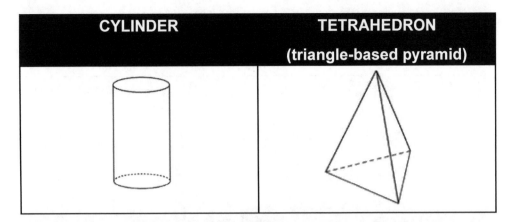

CYLINDER	TETRAHEDRON (triangle-based pyramid)

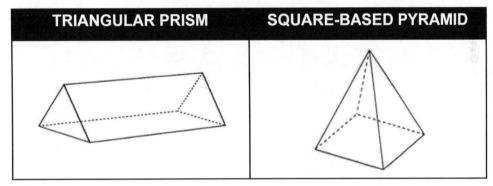

TRIANGULAR PRISM	SQUARE-BASED PYRAMID

When it comes to 3D shapes, there are also some other **KEY WORDS** that you need to be aware of:

- Face
- Vertex
- Edge

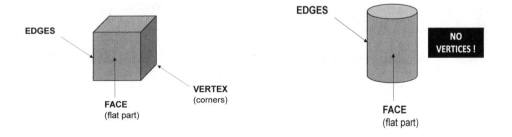

3D NETS

The **NET** of a shape is what the shape would look like if it was opened out flat.

There is often more than one net for each solid shape.

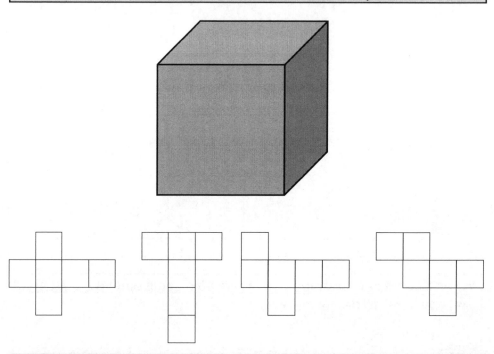

If you fold along all of the lines of the nets above, and then build it, you would end up with the cubed shape.

It is important that you do NOT forget about the hidden faces. In the above 3D shape, you can only see 3 faces. But in actual fact, there are 6 faces!

The cubed nets show how many faces the 3D shape ACTUALLY has, even though some of the shape is hidden.

Below I have drawn some other 3D shapes, with their nets.

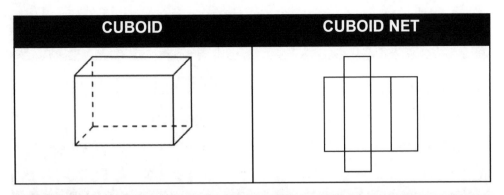

CUBOID | **CUBOID NET**

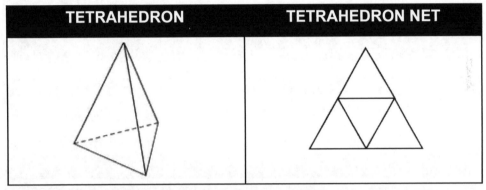

TETRAHEDRON | **TETRAHEDRON NET**

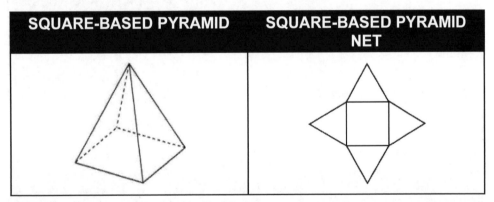

SQUARE-BASED PYRAMID | **SQUARE-BASED PYRAMID NET**

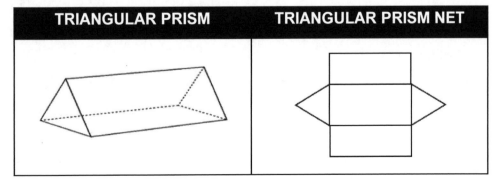

TRIANGULAR PRISM | **TRIANGULAR PRISM NET**

SURFACE AREA

The **SURFACE AREA** is the total area of all of the **FACES.**

To work out the surface area of a 3D shape, you can either:

Work out the area of each face, and then add them all together.

OR

Draw out the net of the 3D shape, and work out the area of the net.

SURFACE AREA = AREA OF THE NET

Let's take a look at some examples of how to work out the surface area of a 3D shape.

CUBOID	HOW TO WORK OUT SURFACE AREA
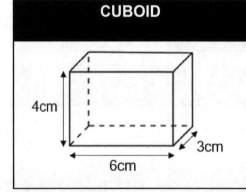 4cm · 6cm · 3cm	• 2(4 x 3) = 24cm² (the sides) • 2(6 x 4) = 48cm² (front and back) • 2(3 x 6) = 36cm² (top and bottom) So, 24 + 48 + 36 = 108cm²

SQUARE-BASED PYRAMID	HOW TO WORK OUT SURFACE AREA
9cm · 6cm	• Area of square = 6 x 6 = 36cm² • Area of triangle = ½ x 6 x 9 = 27cm² • There are 4 triangles = 27 x 4 = 108cm² So, 36 + 108 = 144cm²

TRIANGULAR PRISM	HOW TO WORK OUT SURFACE AREA
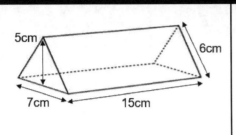	• Area of bottom rectangle = 15 x 7 = 105cm² • Area of side rectangles = 2(15 x 6) = 180cm² • Area of triangles = 2(½ x 7 x 5) = 35cm² So, 105 + 180 + 35 = 320cm²

ACTIVITY TIME!

Below I have drawn a square-based pyramid. Now, I would like you to draw out its net, and then work out its surface area.

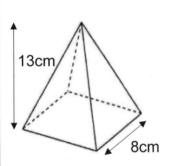

Question Time!

QUESTION 1

Match the 3D shapes with their correct name.

Tetrahedron   Cylinder   Hexagonal   Triangular   Cuboid
                                       prism   prism

QUESTION 2

If the statement is true, put a ✓ in the box. If the statement is false, put a ✗ in the box.

a) Every 3D shape has only one net.

b) A prism is a 3D shape where the two end faces are the same.

c) A square-based pyramid has one square face and four triangular faces.

d) The corners of a shape are also called vertices.

QUESTION 3

For the following 3D shape, draw its net.

a) PENTAGONAL PRISM

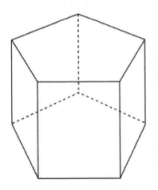

PENTAGONAL PRISM NET

b) CUBE

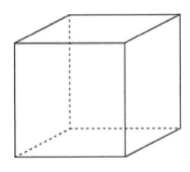

CUBE NET

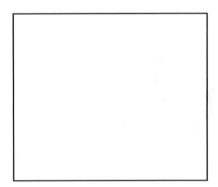

c) TRIANGULAR PRISM

TRIANGULAR PRISM NET

QUESTION 4

Find the surface area of the following shapes:

a) SQUARE-BASED PYRAMID

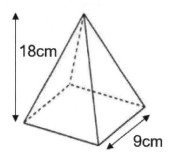

WORK OUT THE SURFACE AREA

b) CUBOID

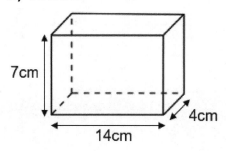

WORK OUT THE SURFACE AREA

c) TRANGULAR PRISM

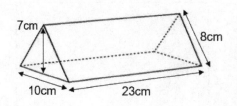

WORK OUT THE SURFACE AREA

QUESTION 5

On the shape below, can you label the three main parts of a solid?

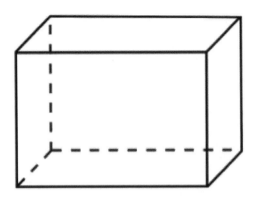

QUESTION 6

For each shape, write how many faces, vertices and edges it has.

	NO. OF FACES	NO. OF VERTICES	NO. OF EDGES

	NO. OF FACES	NO. OF VERTICES	NO. OF EDGES

	NO. OF FACES	NO. OF VERTICES	NO. OF EDGES

Answers

Q1.

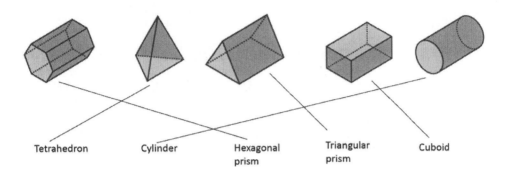

| Tetrahedron | Cylinder | Hexagonal prism | Triangular prism | Cuboid |

Q2.

a) Every 3D shape has only one net.   ✗

b) A prism is a 3D shape where the two end faces are the same. ✓

c) A square-based pyramid has one square face and four triangular faces. ✗

d) The corners of a shape are also called vertices. ✓

Q3.

Pentagonal prism net

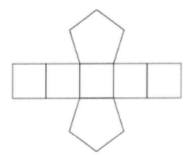

Cube

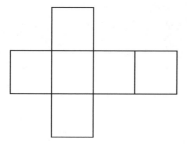

There are lots of different cube nets, so double check your answer!

Triangular prism

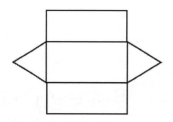

Q4.

a) To work out the area of the square-based pyramid:

- Area of square = 9 x 9 = 81cm²

- Area of triangle = 4(½ x 18 x 9) = 324cm²

- So, 81 + 324 = 405cm²

b) To work out the area of the cuboid:

- Area of top and bottom rectangles = 2(4 x 14) = 112cm²

- Area of side rectangles = 2(4 x 7) = 56cm²

- Area of front and back rectangles = 2(14 x 7) = 196cm²

- So, 112 + 56 + 196 = 364cm²

c) To work out the area of the triangular prism:

- Area of bottom rectangle = 23 x 10 = 230cm²

- Area of side rectangles = 2(23 x 8) = 368cm²

- Area of triangles = 2(½ x 10 x 7) = 70cm²

- So, 230 + 368 + 70 = 668cm²

Q5.

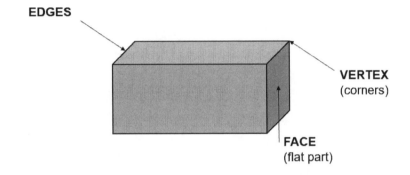

EDGES

VERTEX
(corners)

FACE
(flat part)

Q6.

	NO. OF FACES	NO. OF VERTICES	NO. OF EDGES
	6	8	12

	NO. OF FACES	NO. OF VERTICES	NO. OF EDGES
	3	0	2

	NO. OF FACES	NO. OF VERTICES	NO. OF EDGES
	7	12	18

ANGLES IN SHAPES
(LINES AND ANGLES)

ANGLES IN SHAPES

An angle is a way of measuring a turn. The size of the angle will determine the ANGLE NAME.

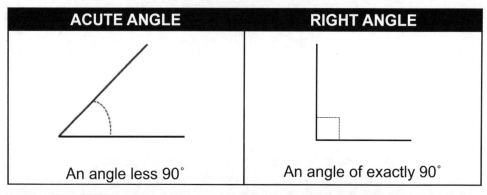

ACUTE ANGLE	RIGHT ANGLE
An angle less 90°	An angle of exactly 90°

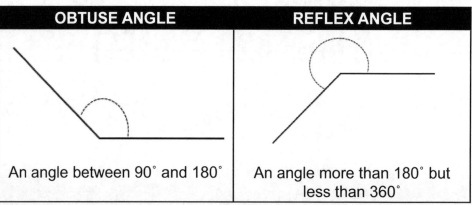

OBTUSE ANGLE	REFLEX ANGLE
An angle between 90° and 180°	An angle more than 180° but less than 360°

These names are often used to describe triangles.

Go back to the chapter on **TRIANGLES** (page 34) for more information on equilateral triangles, isosceles triangles, scalene triangles, and right angle triangles.

ANGLES IN A TRIANGLE

The angles in a triangle will **ALWAYS** add up to 180˚.

EQUILATERAL TRIANGLE

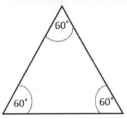

All angles are equal.

Each angle would be 60˚.

ISOSCELES TRIANGLE

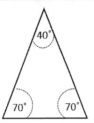

Two angles are of equal size.

SCALENE TRIANGLE

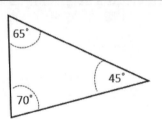

None of the angles are the same size.

RIGHT-ANGLED TRIANGLE

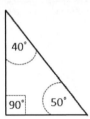

One of the angles will be 90˚.

ANGLES IN A QUADRILATERAL

The angles in a quadrilateral will **ALWAYS** add up to 360°.

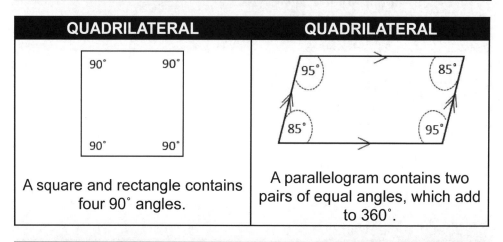

QUADRILATERAL	QUADRILATERAL
A square and rectangle contains four 90° angles.	A parallelogram contains two pairs of equal angles, which add to 360°.

ANGLES OF STRAIGHT LINES AND CIRCLES

The angles on a straight line will **ALWAYS** add up to 180°.

The angles in a circle will **ALWAYS** add up to 360°.

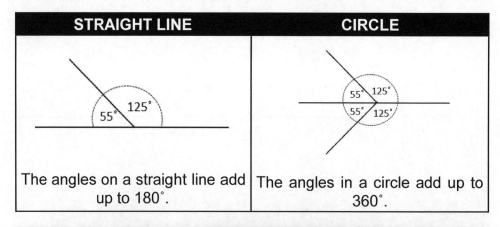

STRAIGHT LINE	CIRCLE
The angles on a straight line add up to 180°.	The angles in a circle add up to 360°.

ANGLE NOTATIONS

Sometimes, you may be asked to talk about a particular angle.

In this instance, the best way to do this is via angle notation. Angle notation uses three letters to describe which angle you are talking about.

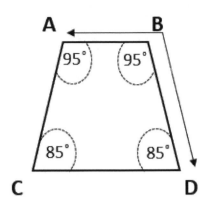

- If you was talking about angle B, you could describe the angle as **ABD** = 95°.

- If you was talking about angle C, you could describe the angle as **ACD** = 85°.

The middle letter in the notation is the actual angle, the other letters tell you which two lines join to make this angle.

Question Time!

QUESTION 1

What is the missing angle?

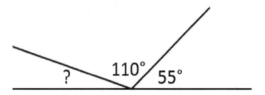

QUESTION 2

Calculate the size of angle **Q** in the diagram.

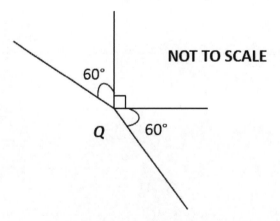

NOT TO SCALE

QUESTION 3

For the following statements, circle whether it is **true** or **false**.

a) An isosceles triangle will always have two angles of the exact same size.

TRUE / FALSE

b) The angles in a circle add up to 180˚.

TRUE / FALSE

c) An obtuse angle is between 180˚ and 360˚.

TRUE / FALSE

QUESTION 4

Link the *types* of angles with their descriptions.

Acute	An angle of 90°.
Obtuse	An angle between 90° and 180°.
Right-angle	An angle less than 90°.
Reflex	An angle greater than 180°.

QUESTION 5

Calculate angle *x*.

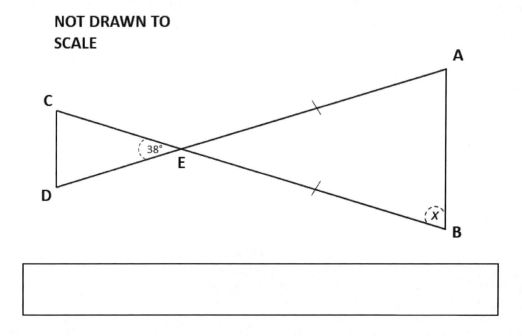

NOT DRAWN TO
SCALE

QUESTION 6

Work out the angle labelled **X**.

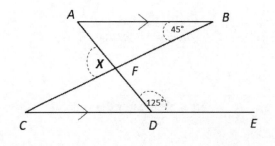

AB and **CE** are parallel lines
Angle **ABC** = 45°
Angle **FDE** = 125°

QUESTION 7

Work out the value of *x*.

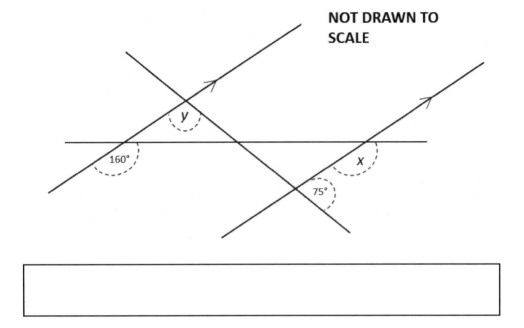

NOT DRAWN TO SCALE

Answers

Q1.

15°

- Angles in a straight line = 180°
- 180 – 110 – 55 = 15°

Q2.

150°

- Angles in a circle = 360°
- 360 – 90 – 60 – 60 = 150°

Q3.

a) An isosceles triangle will always have two angles of the exact same size.

TRUE

b) The angles in a circle add up to 180°.

FALSE

c) An obtuse angle is between 180° and 360°.

FALSE

Q4.

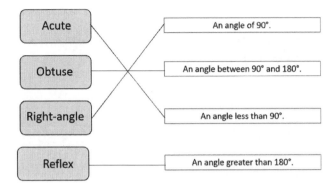

Q5.

71°

- The angle 38° is the same for the opposite angle.
- Angles in a triangle = 180°
- 180 − 38 = 142
- The triangle is an isosceles triangles (indicated by the two dashes on the lines) which means the two angles are of equal size.
- 142 ÷ 2 = 71°

Q6.

100°

- Angle BCD = 45°
- Angle ADC = 55°
- 180 − 80 = 100°

Q7.

160°

* Angle x is on parallel lines with the angle marked 160°. Therefore, these two angles would be of the same size.

MEASURING AND DRAWING ANGLES
ANGLES
(LINES AND ANGLES)

MEASURING ANGLES

It is important that you know how to measure angles with accuracy.

TO MEASURE WITH PRECISION, YOU WILL NEED A PROTRACTOR.

The first thing you should learn is how to read a protractor.

Begin by positioning the protractor along one of the base lines of the shape.

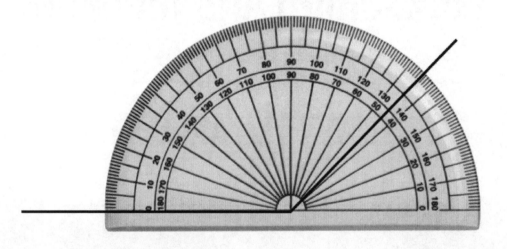

Starting with the line beginning with 0, start counting the steps to see what number the line goes through.

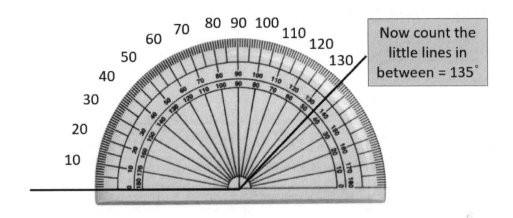

The angle of the lines is 135°.

The angle is **NOT** 45°.

Always remember to begin counting from the zero.

ACTIVITY TIME!

Work out the angle size for the following shapes.

DRAWING ANGLES

It is important that you know how to draw angles

with accuracy.

TO DRAW WITH PRECISION, YOU WILL NEED A PROTRACTOR.

Begin by drawing your base line.

Place your protractor on the straight line, with the end of the line exactly in the middle of the protractor (like shown below).

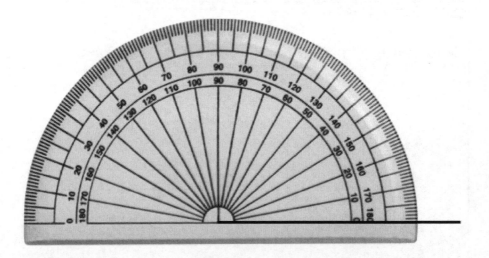

Draw a small dot (or little line) next to the angle that you are trying to find.

Remember, start counting from the number zero. Make sure you are using the right scale on the protractor (**ALWAYS** begin with 0).

Let's say you are trying to draw the angle of 165°.

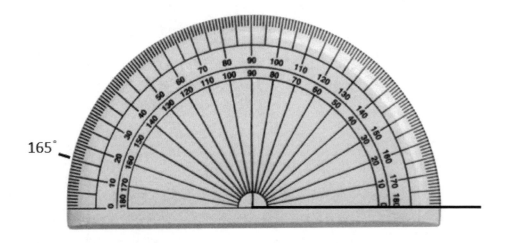

165°

Remove the protractor, and using a ruler, join up the line you have just drawn to the end point of the base line (the end point that was in the middle of the protractor).

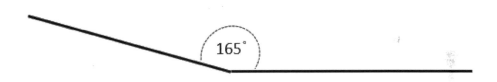

165°

Question Time!

QUESTION 1

Below is a triangle.

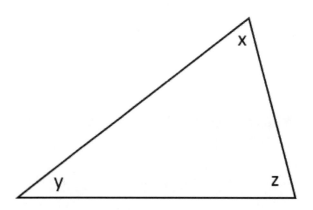

a) Using a protractor, calculate the angle *x*.

b) Using a protractor, calculate the angle *y*.

c) Using a protractor, calculate the angle *z*.

d) What mathematical term can be used to describe the type of triangle?

QUESTION 2

Calculate the following angles:

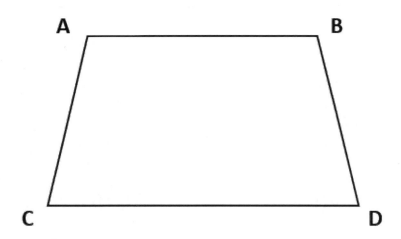

Angle A = _____

Angle B = _____

Angle C = _____

Angle D = _____

QUESTION 3

Draw a triangle with the following angles: **75°   65°   40°**

QUESTION 4

Make an accurate drawing where the base of the triangle is 6cm, with two angles of 48° and 64°.

QUESTION 5

On the shape below, measure each angle.

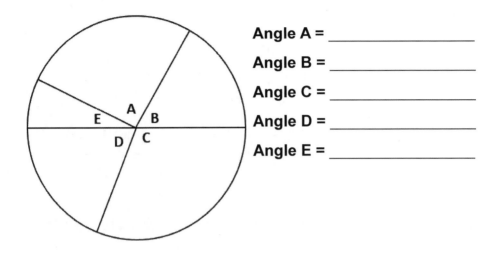

Angle A = _____

Angle B = _____

Angle C = _____

Angle D = _____

Angle E = _____

QUESTION 6

Using a protractor, measure the three angles of the triangle.

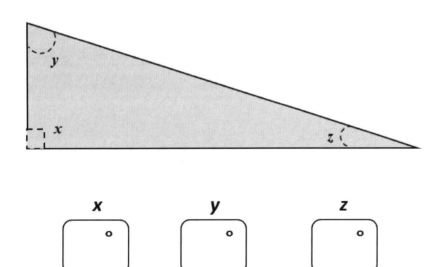

x

y

z

QUESTION 7

Below is a triangle (NOT drawn to scale)

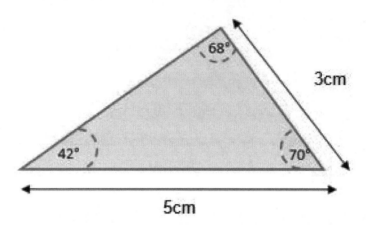

Using a ruler and a protractor, draw out the correct scale of the triangle.

Answers

Q1.

a) Angle x = 67°

b) Angle y = 38°

c) Angle z = 75°

d) Scalene triangle

Q2.

Angle A = 104°

Angle B = 104°

Angle C = 76°

Angle D = 76°

Q3.

Your triangle should look something like this:

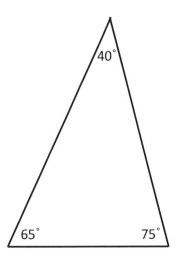

Q4.

- The base line needs to be drawn 6cm in length.

- One of the angles needs to be 48°.

- One of the angles needs to be 64°.

Q5.

Angle A = 93°

Angle B = 61°

Angle C = 112°

Angle D = 68°

Angle E = 26°

Q6.

Angle x = 90°

Angle y = 72 °

Angle z = 18°

Q7.

- Draw the base line 5cm in length.

- You now need to plot the 42° and 70° angle, bearing in mind the length of each side.

INTERIOR AND EXTERIOR ANGLES

ANGLES

(LINES AND ANGLES)

INTERIOR AND EXTERIOR ANGLES OF REGULAR POLYGONS

INTERIOR angles are angles INSIDE the shape.

EXTERIOR angles are angles outside of the shape.

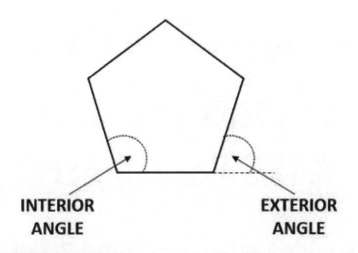

INTERIOR ANGLE

EXTERIOR ANGLE

THE SUM OF INTERIOR AND EXTERIOR ANGLE = 180˚.

THE SUM OF EXTERIOR ANGLES (REGULAR POLYGONS ONLY) = 360˚.

To work out the interior and exterior angles of a REGULAR polygon:

EXTERIOR ANGLE	INTERIOR ANGLE
Exterior angle = $\dfrac{360°}{N}$ N is the number of sides of the shape	Use the exterior angle to work out the interior angle: **Interior angle = 180° - exterior angle**

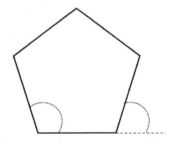

The **EXTERIOR ANGLE** of this regular pentagon is:

$$\frac{360}{5 \textbf{ (number of sides)}} = 72°$$

So that means, the **INTERIOR ANGLE** would be:

180 – 72 = 108°

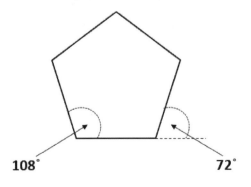

108°   72°

INTERIOR AND EXTERIOR ANGLES OF REGULAR AND IRREGULAR POLYGONS

To work out the interior and exterior angles of ANY polygon:

INTERIOR ANGLE	EXTERIOR ANGLE
To work out the sum of interior angles, you should use this formula: **(n – 2) x 180˚**	Use the interior angle to work out the exterior angle: **Exterior angle = 180˚ - interior angle**

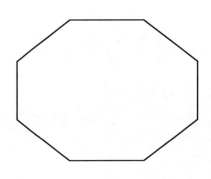

To work out the sum of the interior angles:

- (8-2) x 180º = 1,080º

- So an octagon has a sum of 1,080º angles

To work out the exterior angles:

- 180º - interior angle

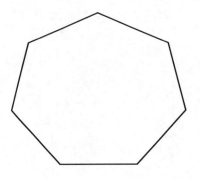

To work out the sum of the interior angles:

- (7-2) x 180º = 900º

- So a heptagon has a sum of 900º angles

To work out the exterior angles:

- 180º - interior angle

Question Time!

QUESTION 1

What is the total sum of interior angles in the shape below?

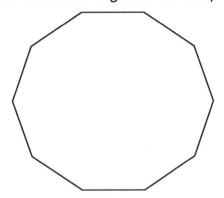

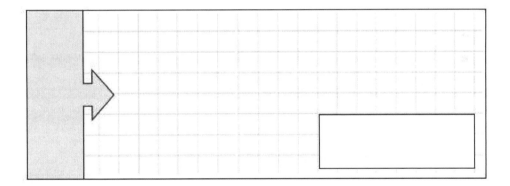

QUESTION 2

Work out whether the statements below are **true** or **false.**

a) The sum of interior angles will always add up to 360˚.

TRUE / FALSE

b) An interior angle in a regular pentagon would is 108˚.

TRUE / FALSE

c) The exterior angles are the angles on the outside of the shape.

TRUE / FALSE

QUESTION 3

Find the interior and exterior angles of a regular nonagon.

_____

_____

_____

_____

QUESTION 4

Work out angle X.

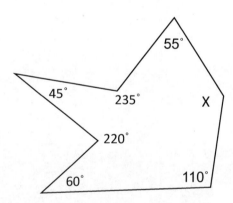

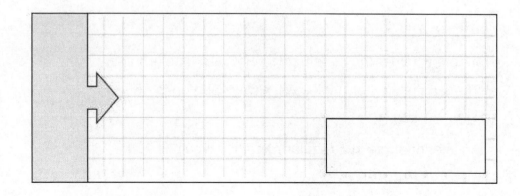

Answers

Q1.

The sum of interior angles of a ten-sided shape = 1,440

- $(10 - 2) \times 180 = 1,440°$

Q2.

a) The sum of interior angles will always add up to $360°$.

FALSE

b) An interior angle in a regular pentagon would be $108°$.

TRUE

c) The exterior angles are the angles on the outside of the shape.

TRUE

Q3.

Interior angle = $140°$ Exterior angle = $40°$

- $(9 - 2) \times 180° = 1,260°$
- $1,260° \div 9 = 140°$
- So, the interior angles of a regular nonagon is $140°$.
- That means the exterior angle is $180 - 140 = 40°$

Q4.

$175°$

- Seven-sided shape = $(7 - 2) \times 180° = 900°$

- $900 - 55 - 235 - 45 - 220 - 60 - 110 = 175°$
- So the missing angle is $175°$

TYPES OF LINES
(LINES AND ANGLES)

PARALLEL LINES

Parallel lines are lines which are going in the exact same direction.

These lines NEVER touch, and are ALWAYS the same distance away from each other.

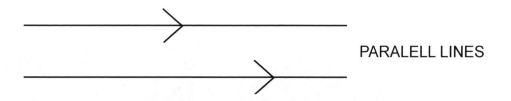

PARALELL LINES

If a diagonal line is positioned through these parallel lines, the angles for each line will be the same. (Shown bottom left).

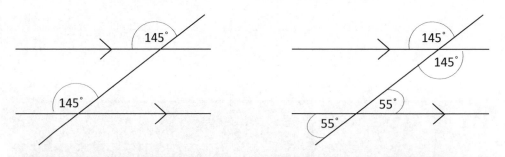

Vertically opposite angles are also the same. (Shown top right).

PERPENDICULAR LINES

Perpendicular lines are lines which meet at a right angle (90°).

These lines ALWAYS touch, and ALWAYS form a 90° angle.

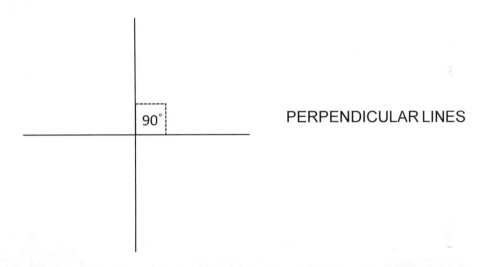

PERPENDICULAR LINES

'Z' LINES

If a 'Z' line is drawn, that means that ALTERNATE angles are the same size.

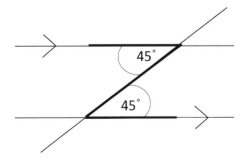

'F' LINES

If an 'F' line is drawn, that means the CORRESPONDING angles are the same size.

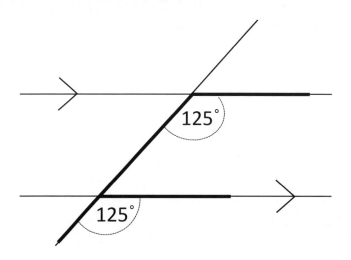

'C' AND 'U' LINES

If a 'C' or 'U' line is drawn, that means the ALLIED angles will add up to 180°.

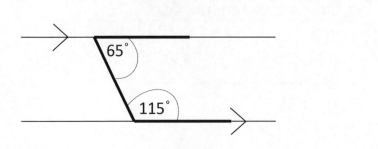
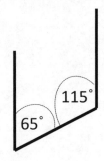

LINES OF SYMMETRY

Lines of symmetry is where you can draw one (or more) lines on a shape, which act as a mirror.

Whatever is on one side of the mirror line is reflected EXACTLY the same on the other side of the mirror line.

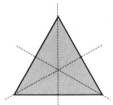 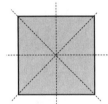 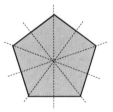 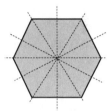

| 3 lines of symmetry | 4 lines of symmetry | 5 lines of symmetry | 6 lines of symmetry |

When working out how many lines of symmetry a shape has, remember not to count the same line twice!

ROTATIONAL SYMMETRY

Rotational symmetry is when you can rotate the whole shape, and have it still look exactly the same.

| Rotational symmetry order 1 | Rotational symmetry order 2 | Rotational symmetry order 3 | Rotational symmetry order 4 |

Question Time!

QUESTION 1

Which lines are perpendicular?

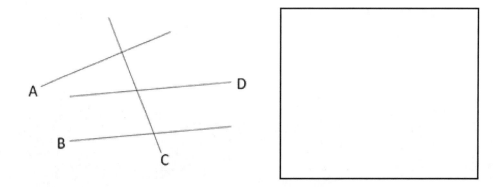

QUESTION 2

Which lines are parallel?

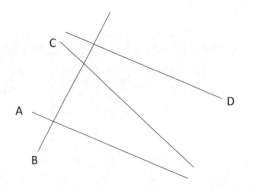
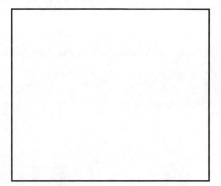

QUESTION 3

Draw a line on the grid to illustrate parallel lines.

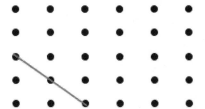

QUESTION 4

Draw a line from point A to illustrate perpendicular lines.

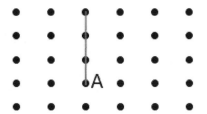

QUESTION 5

What type of lines are the ones with the arrows?

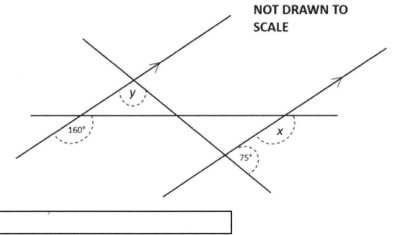

QUESTION 6

Work out the value of x.

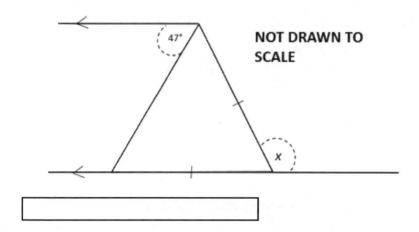

NOT DRAWN TO SCALE

QUESTION 7

AB and CD are parallel straight lines.

EF and GH are equal.

Work out the value of x.

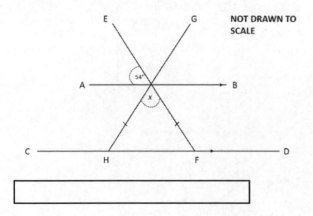

NOT DRAWN TO SCALE

QUESTION 8

Lines AB and CD are parallel.

Lines GH and EF are the same length.

a) Work out the value of x.

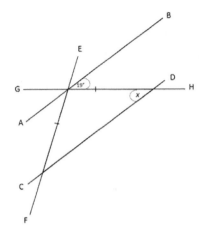

b) Using appropriate terminology, explain your answer to part a.

Answers

Q1.

A and C

• Only the lines A and C are perpendicular to one another.

Q2.

A and D

• Only lines A and D are parallel to one another.

Q3.

*Your answer should look something like this:

Q4.

*Your answer should look something like this:

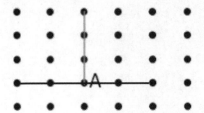

Q5.

Parallel lines.

Q6.

94°

- 47° is an alternate angle.
- The triangle is an isosceles triangle, which means two angles are 47°. So, 180 − 47 − 47 = 86
- So, angle x is 180 − 86 = 94°

Q7.

Angle x = 72°

- 180 − 54 − 54 = 72

Q8.

Angle x = 19°

- Lines AB and CD are parallel. This means the angle of 19° is equivalent to angle x.

H O W   A R E   Y O U   G E T T I N G   O N ?

PERIMETER, AREA AND VOLUME

HOW TO WORK OUT PERIMETER

The perimeter of a shape is the total distance AROUND the edge of the shape.

To work out the perimeter:

Add up the lengths of all the sides of the shape.

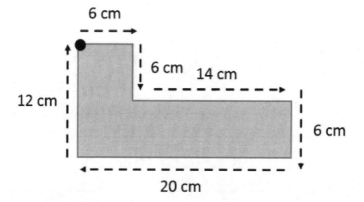

EXAMPLE

How to work out the perimeter of the shape above:

- **Step 1** – draw a black dot on one of the corners. This will be your starting point, and it will allow you to count accurately.

- **Step 2** – now, work your way around the shape, adding up all of the sides.

- **Step 3** – the arrows drawn on the above example are a great way to show you which sides have been counted.

- **Step 4** – 6 + 6 +14 + 6 + 20 + 12 = 64.

- **Step 5** – So, the perimeter of the above shape is 64 cm.

Sometimes, you may be asked to work out the perimeter of a shape, but side lengths are missing. This is where you will need to work out each side length before working out the perimeter.

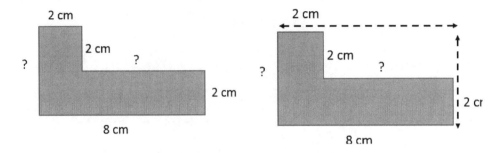

Here we are missing two sides.

Let's work out the vertical side first. This can be worked out by adding the other two vertical sides together.

So, the missing vertical side will be 4cm. (By adding the 2cm and 2cm as shown above).

The horizontal missing side can be worked out by subtracting the 2cm from the 8cm. So 8 − 2 = 6.

So, 2 + 2 + 6 + 2 + 8 + 4 = 24 cm.

ACTIVITY TIME!

Work out the perimeter of the following shape.

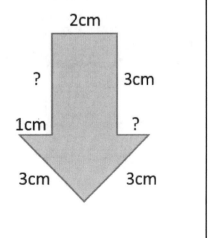

HOW TO WORK OUT AREA

The area of a shape is the amount of SURFACE area it covers.

To work out the area:

To work out the area of a shape, you will need to learn a few area **FORMULAS**.

AREA (Squares and rectangles)	AREA FORMULA	EXAMPLE
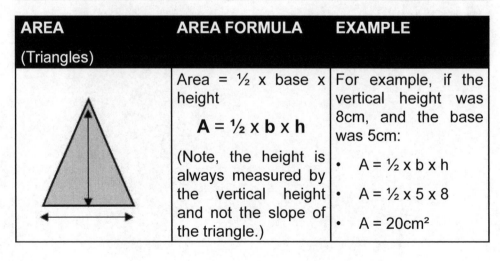	Area = length x width $$A = l \times w$$	For example, if the length of the rectangle was 7cm, and the width was 4cm: • $A = l \times w$ • $A = 7 \times 4$ • $A = 28cm^2$

AREA (Triangles)	AREA FORMULA	EXAMPLE
	Area = ½ x base x height $$A = ½ \times b \times h$$ (Note, the height is always measured by the vertical height and not the slope of the triangle.)	For example, if the vertical height was 8cm, and the base was 5cm: • $A = ½ \times b \times h$ • $A = ½ \times 5 \times 8$ • $A = 20cm^2$

AREA	AREA FORMULA	EXAMPLE
(Trapezium)		
	Area = ½ x (side a + side b) x height **A = ½ x (a + b) x h**	For example, if side a was 3cm, side b was 9cm, and the height was 6cm: • A = ½ x (a + b) x h • A = ½ x (3 + 9) x 6 • A = ½ x 12 x 6 • A = 36cm²

AREA	AREA FORMULA	EXAMPLE
(Parallelogram)		
	Area = base x vertical height **A = b x h**	For example, if the base was 11cm, and the vertical height was 5cm: • A = b x h • A = 11 x 5 • A = 55cm²

AREA OF A COMPOUND SHAPE

Finding the area of one shape is easy, finding the area of a compound shape is a bit trickier.

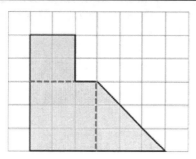

Each square = 1 cm

How to work out the area of this compound shape:

- **Step 1** = break up the shape. You should realise there are 2 squares and a triangle.

- **Step 2** = area of top square = 2 x 2 = 4 cm²

- **Step 3** = area of bottom square = 3 x 3 = 9 cm²

- **Step 4** = area of triangle = 3 x 3 ÷ 2 = 4.5 cm²

- **Step 5** = add up all of the totals = 4 + 9 + 4.5 = 17.5 cm².

HOW TO WORK OUT VOLUME

Volume is the AMOUNT OF SPACE which is taken up.

When dealing with volume, you will ALWAYS be dealing with 3D shapes.

1 cube
(1 x 1 x 1)

2 cubes
(2 x 1 x 1)

4 cubes
(2 x 2 x 1)

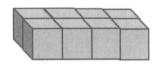
8 cubes
(4 x 2 x 1)

VOLUME (Squares and rectangles)	VOLUME FORMULA	EXAMPLE
	Volume = length x width x height $$V = l \times w \times h$$	For example, if the length of the rectangle was 8cm, the width was 4cm and the height was 6cm: • V = l x w x h • V = 8 x 4 x 6 • A = 192cm³

VOLUME (Prisms)	VOLUME FORMULA	EXAMPLE
	Volume = cross-sectional area x length $$V = a \times l$$	For example, if the triangle had a height of 5cm and base of 6cm, and the length of the prism was 7cm: • $V = a \times l$ • $V = 15 \times 7$ • $A = 105cm^3$

Question Time!

QUESTION 1

Look at the shape below.

SCALE = 1cm x 1cm

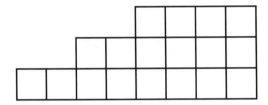

a) Work out the perimeter.

b) Work out the area. Give the correct units.

QUESTION 2

Work out the volume of the shape below, given that each cube is 1x1x1

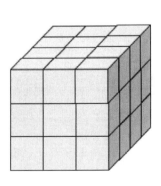

QUESTION 3

Work out the area of the total shape. You must show your working out.

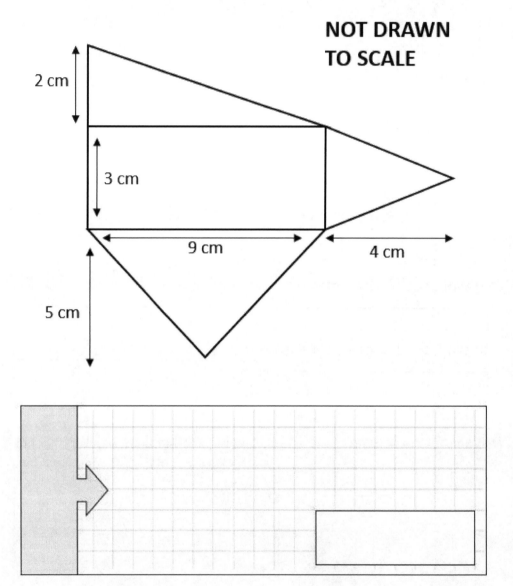

NOT DRAWN TO SCALE

QUESTION 4

Work out the area of this parallelogram.

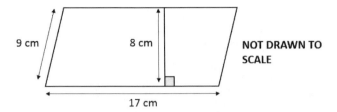

9 cm   8 cm   NOT DRAWN TO SCALE

17 cm

QUESTION 5

Work out the perimeter of this shape.

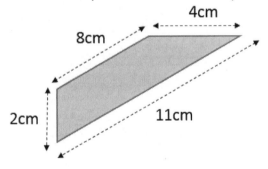

4cm

8cm

2cm   11cm

QUESTION 6

Adam has a rectangular garden. The length of his garden is 18 metres, and the width of his garden is 9 metres. Calculate the perimeter of Adam's garden.

QUESTION 7

Work out the area of this shape.

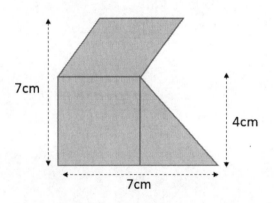

QUESTION 8

Given that each cube is 1cm, work out the volume of this shape.

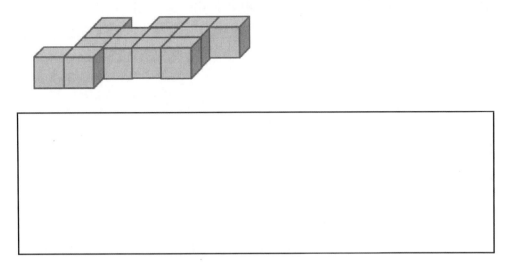

QUESTION 9

Find the volume of the triangular prism below.

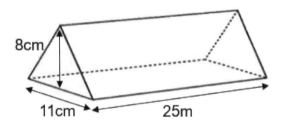

8cm

11cm   25m

QUESTION 10

The cross-sectional area of a heptagonal prism is 49cm². The length of the prism is 8cm. Work out the volume of the heptagonal prism.

QUESTION 11

A cylinder has a volume of 117cm³. The length is 13cm. What is the area of one of the cross-sections?

QUESTION 12

The diagram below shows the net of a square-based pyramid.

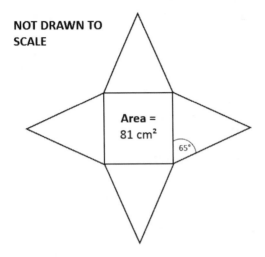

NOT DRAWN TO SCALE

Area = 81 cm²

65°

a) If the height of the triangle is 8cm, work out the area of one of the triangles.

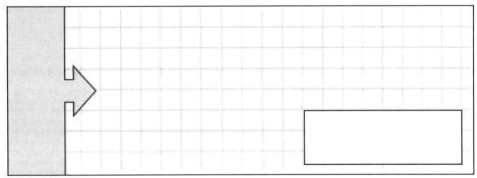

b) Work out the total area of the whole shape.

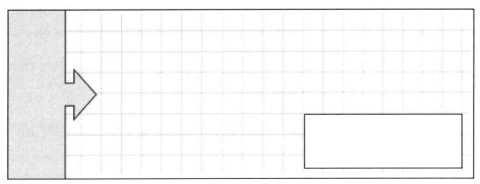

Answers

Q1.

a) 22cm

$1 + 2 + 1 + 2 + 1 + 4 + 3 + 8 = 22$

b) 18cm²

$(4 \times 3) + (2 \times 2) + (2 \times 1)\ 12 + 4 + 2 = 18cm²$

Q2.

36cm³

- $3 \times 3 \times 4 = 36cm³$

Q3.

64.5cm²

- Top triangle = $½ \times 2 \times 9 = 9$
- Bottom triangle = $½ \times 9 \times 5 = 22.5$
- Side triangle = $½ \times 4 \times 3 = 6$
- Rectangle = $3 \times 9 = 27$
- $9 + 22.5 + 6 + 27 = 64.5cm²$

Q4.

136cm²

- Area of parallelogram = base x height
- Area = $17 \times 8 = 136cm²$

Q5.

25cm

- 8 + 4 + 11 + 2 = 25cm

Q6.

54 metres

- Length of the garden = 18 metres (18 x 2)
- Width of garden = 9 metres (9 x 2)
- 36 + 18 = 54 metres

Q7.

34cm²

- Area of square = 4 x 4 = 16cm²
- Area of triangle = ½ x 3 x 4 = 6cm²
- Area of rhombus = 4 x 3 = 12cm²
- 16 + 6 + 12 = 34cm²

Q8.

14cm³

- There are fourteen 1x1 squares, which means the volume is 14.

Q9.

1,100cm³

- Volume for prism = area of cross-section x length
- Cross-section = ½ x 8 x 11 = 44cm³
- 44 x 25 = 1,100³

Q10.

392cm³

- Area of prism = area of cross-section x length
- 49 x 8 = 392cm³

Q11.

9cm²

- 117 ÷ 13 = 9

Q12.

a) 36cm²

- Each side of the square is 9cm (9 x 9 = 81cm²)
- So, the area of the triangle = ½ x 9 x 8 = 36cm²

b) 225cm²

- Using your answer to part a, you know that the area of one triangle is 36cm²
- There are 4 triangles = 4 x 36 = 144cm²
- You need to add this to the area of the square = 144 + 81 = 225cm²

HOW ARE YOU GETTING ON?

TRANSFORM AND ENLARGE

TRANSFORMATIONS AND ENLARGEMENTS

You need to learn the four TRANSFORMATIONS when it comes to looking at shapes.

The four transformations that you need to know are:

1. Translations

2. Rotations

3. Reflections

4. Enlargements

TRANSLATIONS

When we talk about translating shapes, this basically means **SLIDING** the shape into a new position.

Translations are very easy to understand if you know how the shape has been moved. That is why we must **ALWAYS** say how far along and how far up (or down) the shape has moved.

We describe the movement of the shape using **VECTORS**.

When describing the movement, you will:

1. First describe the movement on the x axis (how many spaces the shape has moved left or right).

2. And then, describe the movement on the y axis (how many spaces the shape has moved up or down).

EXAMPLE

Take a look at the following grid. Triangles A, B and C have all been translated. But, we need to understand how each shape has moved across the page; and to do this we will use vectors.

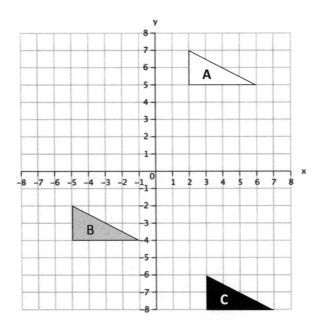

Step 1 = place a black dot on one of the corners on triangle A. Whichever corner of the triangle you have marked, do the same for triangles B and C.

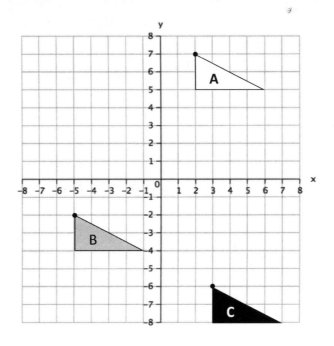

Step 2 = next, work out how triangle A translates to triangle B.

- Using the dotted corner on triangle A, first work out how the triangle has moved sideways.

   The triangle has moved 7 spaces to the left (which means the vector would be -7).

- Next, work out how the triangle has moved up or down.

   The triangle has moved 9 spaces downwards (which means the vector would be -9).

- So the translation by vector from A to B is $\begin{pmatrix} -7 \\ -9 \end{pmatrix}$

Step 3 = next, work out how triangle B translates to triangle C.

- Using the dotted corner on triangle B, first work out how the triangle has moved sideways.

   The triangle has moved 8 spaces to the right (which means the vector would be 8).

- Next, work out how the triangle has moved up or down.

   The triangle has moved 4 spaces downwards (which means the vector would be -4).

- So, the translation by vector from B to C is $\begin{pmatrix} 8 \\ -4 \end{pmatrix}$

REMEMBER

- Moving to the right or up – vector number will be POSITIVE

- Moving to the left or down – vector number will be NEGATIVE

- Describe the x axis first (right or left)

- Describe the y axis second (up or down)

ROTATIONS

Another way you can transform a shape is by **ROTATION.**

When describing a rotation, you will need to know:

1. The direction of rotation (clockwise or anti-clockwise).

2. The angle of rotation (90° or 180°).

3. The centre of rotation.

EXAMPLE

Take a look at the following grid. Triangle A has been rotated to form triangle B.

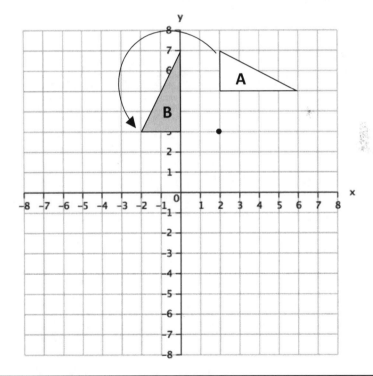

In the above diagram, triangle A has been rotated 90° ANTI-CLOCKWISE.

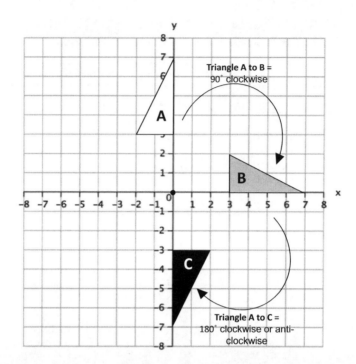

In the above diagram, we are using the centre rotation of (0, 0).

To get from triangle A to triangle B, we have rotated triangle A 90° clockwise.

If you wanted to get from triangle A to triangle C, we can rotate the triangle 180° using the centre rotation vectors. It does not matter whether you go clockwise or anti-clockwise, because you will end up in the same position!

REMEMBER

- Make sure you know the angle of rotation, direction of rotation and/ or the centre of rotation.

- A good way to practise these types of questions is to use **TRACING PAPER**.

- Know the difference between clockwise and anti-clockwise. Clockwise is the direction you will see the hands of a clock moving around in.

REFLECTIONS

Another transformation is using **REFLECTIONS**.

Think of shape reflections as a way of looking into a mirror. Using a mirror line, the object must appear exactly as it does on the other side.

The mirror line can be placed anywhere on an x and y grid.

EXAMPLE

Take a look at the following grid. Triangles A, B and C have all been reflected using mirror lines.

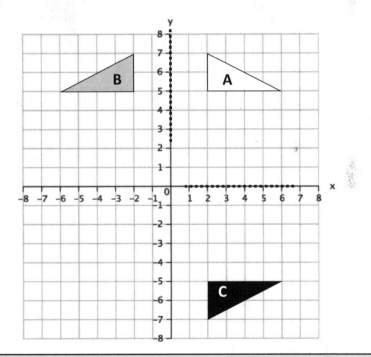

The diagram shows two reflections.

To get from triangle A to triangle B, we have reflected the shape using the y axis.

To get from the triangle A to triangle C, we have reflected the shape using the x axis.

The dotted black lines represent mirrors!

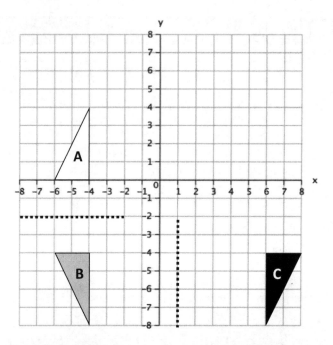

In the diagram above, the mirror line between triangle A and triangle B is y = -2.

The mirror line between triangle B and triangle C is x = 1.

REFLECTIONS

ENLARGEMENTS are a way of transforming the size of a shape.

We can use a **SCALE FACTOR** to work out how the side lengths are changing.

For example, a scale factor of 2 means multiply each side by 2.

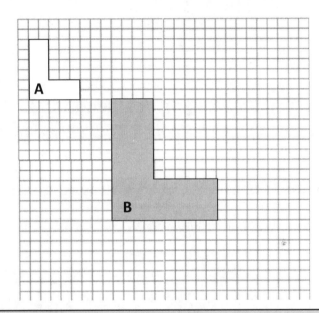

The scale factor of shape A to shape B has a scale factor of 2.

Each side length has been multiplied by 2.

When describing an enlargement, you need to focus on:

1. The scale factor
2. The centre of enlargement.

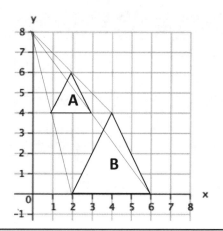

To work out the scale factor:

New length ÷ old length

So the scale factor which transforms triangle A to triangle B is a scale factor of 2.

The centre of enlargement is (0, 8).

To work out the centre of enlargement:

- Draw lines which go through the matching corners of each shape. So, draw a line going through the top corner of triangle A to the top corner of triangle B, and so forth.

- Wherever these lines meet, that is the centre of enlargement.

Question Time!

QUESTION 1

Below is a 1cm by 1cm grid.

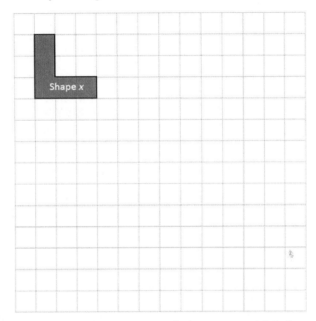

Draw on the grid an enlargement of shape x, which has a scale factor of 3.

QUESTION 2

Explain the difference between rotation, reflection and translation.

_____

_____

_____

_____

QUESTION 3

Describe the transformation that maps shape A onto shape B.

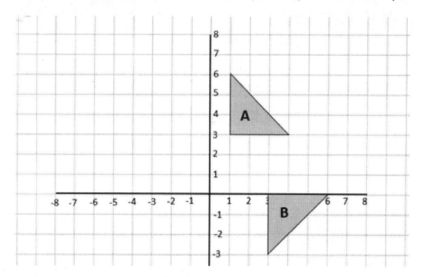

QUESTION 4

Using shape A, rotate 90° anti-clockwise, and draw the image in the top right quarter of the grid (using the black point as a reference). Label this shape 'B'. Next, translate shape B -7 vertically and +3 horizontally. Draw the shape and label 'C'. Next reflect shape C (using the y axis) into the bottom left quadrant of the grid and label 'D'.

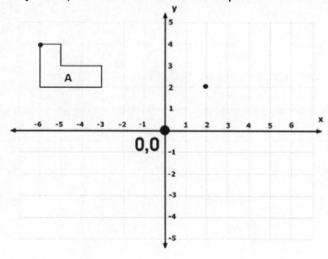

QUESTION 5

Using the black point as reference, rotate the shape clockwise so that the black point has the coordinate (2,2).

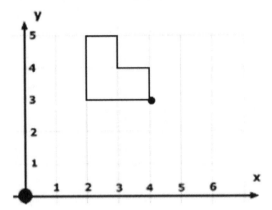

QUESTION 6

Reflect shape A in the y axis. Label this shape 'B'. Using shape B, reflect this horizontally, using the x axis as the mirror line. Label this shape 'C'.

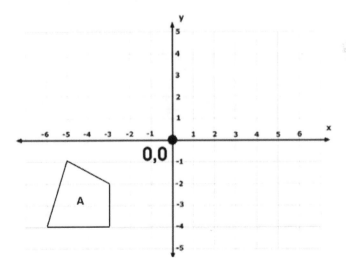

QUESTION 7

Translate shape A using the vectors $\begin{pmatrix} -7 \\ -2 \end{pmatrix}$. Label the new shape 'B'.

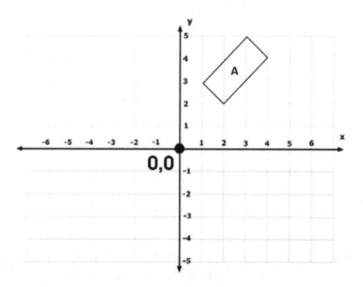

QUESTION 8

Reflect shape A using the x axis. Label the new shape 'B'.

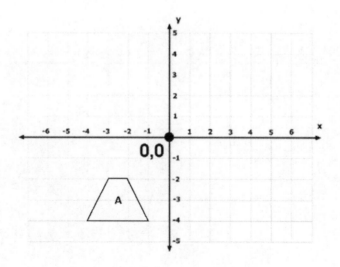

Answers

Q1.

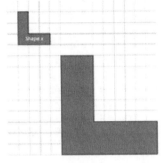

Q2.

Rotation is when a shape is rotated using a particular point. The shape can be rotated clockwise or anti-clockwise, using a particular point called the point of rotation. Reflection is when, if you were to use a mirror, the shape would look exactly the same on the opposite side. Translation is when a shape slides from one position to another; it is neither rotated nor reflected.

Q3.

To get from shape A to shape B, the shape has been rotated 90° clockwise using the point (0,0).

Q4.

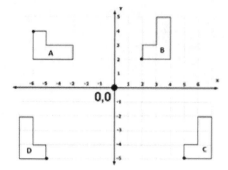

Q5.

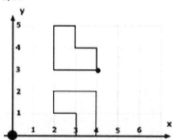

Q6.

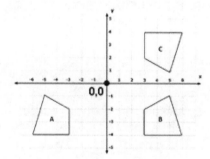

Q7.

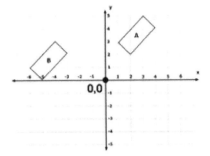

Q8.

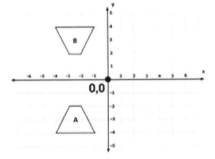

CONSTRUCTIONS

TRANSFORMATIONS AND ENLARGEMENTS

Some maths questions may ask you to construct your own diagram.

A ruler, protractor and compasses are often required for these types of questions.

HOW TO CONSTRUCT A TRIANGLE

If you are asked to construct a triangle knowing ALL of the side lengths:

EXAMPLE 1

Construct a triangle (ABC) where AB = 4cm, BC = 3cm, AC = 5cm.

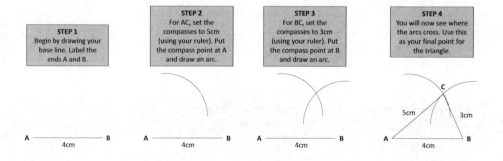

STEP 1
Begin by drawing your base line. Label the ends A and B.

STEP 2
For AC, set the compasses to 5cm (using your ruler). Put the compass point at A and draw an arc.

STEP 3
For BC, set the compasses to 3cm (using your ruler). Put the compass point at B and draw an arc.

STEP 4
You will now see where the arcs cross. Use this as your final point for the triangle.

Note:

The example is not drawn to scale, and should only be used as an example of how to work out constructions.

If you are asked to construct a triangle knowing TWO side lengths and ONE angle size.

EXAMPLE 2

Construct a triangle (ABC) where AB = 5cm, AC = 3cm, and angle ABC = 30°.

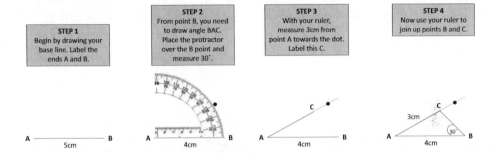

HOW TO CONSTRUCT A BISECTOR OF AN ANGLE

If you are asked to construct a bisector of an angle, you need to know how to divide up the angle.

Remember, the bisector of an angle basically means 'exactly half'.

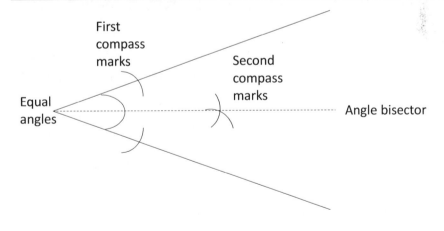

HOW TO CONSTRUCT A PERPENDICULAR BISECTOR OF A STRAIGHT LINE

If you are asked to construct a perpendicular bisector of a straight line AB, that means you need to create a line which makes a right angle passing through the midpoint of the line AB.

Remember, the bisector of an angle basically means 'exactly half'.

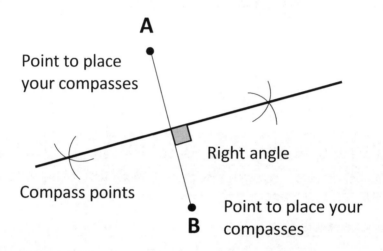

Point to place your compasses

Right angle

Compass points

Point to place your compasses

A

B

- **STEP 1**

Begin by placing your compasses the same distance apart as line AB.

- **STEP 2**

Place your compass on point A. Draw an arc to either side of the line AB.

- **STEP 3**

Leaving the compasses that set distance apart, move the compass to point B, and draw an arc either side of the line.

- **STEP 4**

You should see that on each side of the line, the two arcs meet. Draw your line through the adjoining arcs, to create the perpendicular bisector.

Question Time!

QUESTION 1

Construct a triangle ABC, where AB = 6cm, BC = 4 cm and AC = 5cm.

QUESTION 2

Construct a triangle ABC, where AB = 8cm, CAB = 60° and CBA = 40°.

QUESTION 3

For the angle below, draw an angle bisector. <u>You should leave all of your working out.</u>

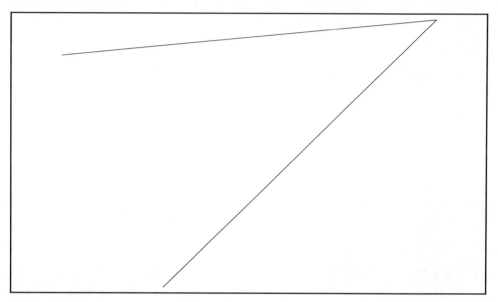

QUESTION 4

Using the line AB, draw a perpendicular bisector. <u>You should leave all of your working out.</u>

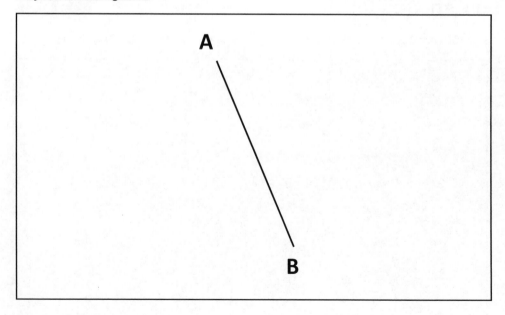

Answers

Q1.

Your answer should look something like this:

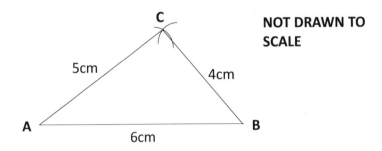

NOT DRAWN TO SCALE

Q2.

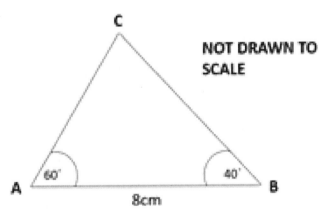

NOT DRAWN TO SCALE

- Line AB is 8cm.
- Place the protractor on point A and work out 60°. Mark that point.
- Place the protractor on point B and work out 40°. Mark that point.
- Where the two points meet, this is where your triangle will form.

Q3.

NOT DRAWN TO SCALE

Q4.

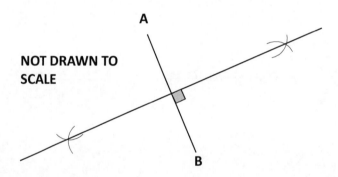

NOT DRAWN TO SCALE

A

B

INTRODUCTION TO PYTHAGORAS

PYTHAGORAS' THEROM

Pythagoras' Theorem can be used to find ANY length of a triangle.

PYTHAGORAS' THEOREM FORMULA
$$a^2 + b^2 = c^2$$

When it comes to Pythagoras, there are a few things that you need to be aware of:

- Pythagoras' Theorem can only be applied to **RIGHT-ANGLED TRIANGLES**.

- Two sides of the triangle will always be known, and you will need to work out the third length.

- Make sure that your answer **LOOKS** sensible!

- The longest side of the triangle is called the **HYPOTENUSE**, and this side is always opposite the right angle.

- The hypotenuse is equal to the sum of the squared numbers for the other sides of the triangle.

EXAMPLE 1

Find the length AB in the triangle.

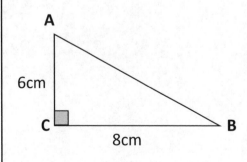

AB = hypotenuse

- $6^2 + 8^2 = AB^2$
- $36 + 64 = 100$
- $100 = AB^2$
- $AB = \sqrt{100} = 10$ cm

EXAMPLE 2

Find the length BC in the triangle. Write your answer to 2 decimal places.

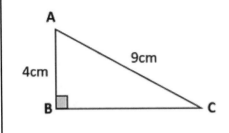

- $BC^2 + 4^2 = 9^2$
- $BC^2 + 16 = 81$
- $BC^2 = 81 - 16 = 65$
- $AB = \sqrt{65} = 8.0622$ cm
- To 2 decimal places = 8.06 cm

EXAMPLE 3

Find the length BC in the triangle. Write your answer to 1 decimal place.

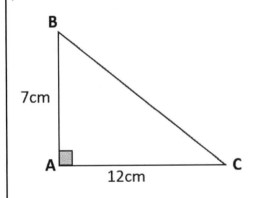

BC = hypotenuse

- $7^2 + 12^2 = BC^2$
- $49 + 144 = 193$
- $193 = BC^2$
- $BC = \sqrt{193} = 13.892$ cm
- To 1 decimal place = 13.9 cm

Key things to remember:

- If you are trying to find the longest side, you will ADD the two squared numbers.

- If you are trying to find one of the shorter sides, you will SUBTRACT the smaller one from the larger one.

- Square the two numbers you are given. There is a squared button on a calculator!

x^2

- Remember to find the square root! There is a squared root button on a calculator!

Question Time!

QUESTION 1

Find the side length of AB. Write your answer to 2 decimal places.

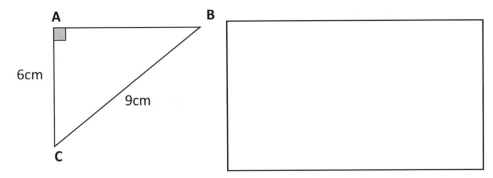

QUESTION 2

Find the side length of AB. Write your answer to 1 decimal place.

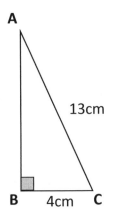
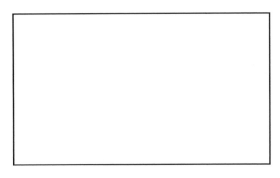

QUESTION 3

Find the side length of BC. Write your answer to 1 decimal place.

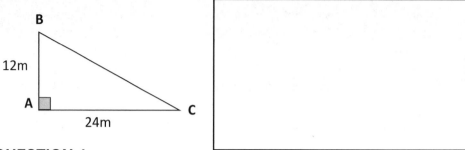

QUESTION 4

One of the short sides of a triangle measures 5cm. The other short side measures 8cm. Work out the length of the hypotenuse to two decimal places.

QUESTION 5

For the following statements, circle whether they are **true** or **false.**

a) The correct formula to work out Pythagoras' Theorem is $a^2 + b^2 = c^2$.

TRUE / FALSE

b) To find the longest side, you need to subtract the two shorter sides.

TRUE / FALSE

c) If the hypotenuse of the triangle is 7.6cm and the shortest side of the triangle is 3cm, that means the other side of the triangle is 7cm.

TRUE / FALSE

d) Pythagoras' Theorem works with any triangle.

TRUE / FALSE

Answers

Q1.

6.71cm

- $AB^2 + 6^2 = 9^2$
- $AB^2 + 36 = 81$
- $AB^2 = 81 - 36 = 45$
- $AB = \sqrt{45} = 6.708$
- To 2 decimal places = 6.71cm

Q2.

12.4cm

- $AB^2 + 4^2 = 13^2$
- $AB^2 + 16 = 169$
- $AB^2 = 169 - 16 = 153$
- $AB = \sqrt{153} = 12.369$
- To 1 decimal place = 12.4cm

Q3.

- 26.8m
- $12^2 + 24^2 = BC^2$
- $144 + 576 = BC^2$
- $720 = BC^2$
- $BC = \sqrt{720} = 26.832$

- To 1 decimal place = 26.8m

Q4.

9.43cm

- $5^2 + 8^2$ = long side^2
- 25 + 64 = long side^2
- 89 = long side^2
- Long side = $\sqrt{89}$ = 9.433
- To 2 decimal places = 9.43cm

Q5.

a) The correct formula to work out Pythagoras' Theorem is $a^2 + b^2 = c^2$.

TRUE

b) To find the longest side, you need to subtract the two shorter sides.

FALSE

c) If the hypotenuse of the triangle is 7.6cm and the shortest side of the triangle is 3cm, that means the other side of the triangle is 7cm.

TRUE

d) Pythagoras' Theorem works with any triangle.

FALSE

HOW ARE YOU GETTING ON?

INTRODUCTION TO TRIGONOMETRY

TRIGONOMETRY

Each side of a triangle has a special name:

HYPOTENUSE, OPPOSITE and ADJACENT

Each one of the names above links two sides and an angle. Again, this only works with **RIGHT-ANGLED TRIANGLES.**

The hypotenuse = the longest side of the triangle.

The opposite = the opposite side to the angle being used (x)

The adjacent = is the other side next to the angle being used.

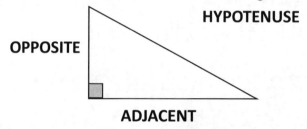

DON'T FORGET:

SOH   CAH   TOA

SOH	CAH	TOA

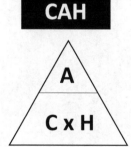 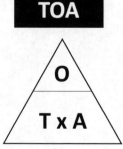

There are three formulas that you need to understand.

$$\text{Sin } x = \frac{Opposite}{Hypotenuse}$$ $$\text{Cos } x = \frac{Adjacent}{Hypotenuse}$$ $$\text{Tan } x = \frac{Opposite}{Adjacent}$$

Key things to remember:

• When you have a question on trigonometry, you should first look at what two sides you have been given. (O,H   A,H   or   O,A)

• From that, you will be able to choose which formula you need to use to solve the question. (**SOH**,   **CAH**,   **TOA**)

• Then using the formula, use the triangles above to show you how to correctly use each formula.

• Cover up the thing you are trying to find, and do the calculation that is left.

EXAMPLE

Work out the length of the opposite side. Give your answer to 1 decimal place.

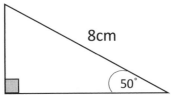

STEP 1

Label the sides.

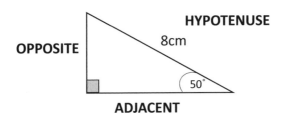

STEP 2

The opposite and the hypotenuse are involved, so the formula we will use is **SOH.**

STEP 3

We are trying to work out O, so cover it up and do the calculation:

$= \mathbf{s}\text{in } 50° \text{ x } 8 = 6.12$

To 1 decimal place = 6.1cm

Question Time!

QUESTION 1

Find the length of AB. Write your answer to 1 decimal place.

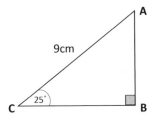

QUESTION 2

Find the length of AC. Write your answer to 1 decimal place.

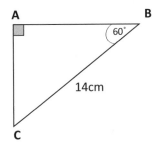

QUESTION 3

Find the length of AC. Write your answer to 1 decimal place.

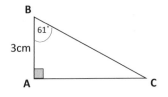

Answers

Q1.

3.8cm

- SOH
- O = S x H
- O = Sin25° x 9 = 3.803
- To 1 decimal place = 3.8cm

Q2.

12.1cm

- SOH
- O = S x H
- O = Sin60° x 14 = 12.124
- To 1 decimal place = 12.1cm

Q3.

5.4cm

- AC is opposite to the angle given and AB is adjacent to it.
- 3 x Tan61 = 5.412
- To 1 decimal place = 5.4cm

NEED A LITTLE EXTRA HELP WITH KEY STAGE THREE (KS3) MATHS?

How2Become have created these other FANTASTIC guides to help you and your child prepare for their Key Stage Three (KS3) Maths assessments.

FOR MORE INFORMATION ON OUR KEY STAGE 3 (KS3) MATHS GUIDES, PLEASE CHECK OUT THE FOLLOWING:

WWW.HOW2BECOME.COM

WANT TO TAKE A LOOK AT OUR KEY STAGE THREE (KS3) ENGLISH GUIDES?

How2Become have created these other FANTASTIC guides to help you and your child prepare for their Key Stage Three (KS3) English assessments.

FOR MORE INFORMATION ON OUR KEY STAGE 3 (KS3) ENGLISH GUIDES, PLEASE CHECK OUT THE FOLLOWING:

WWW.HOW2BECOME.COM

Get Access To

FREE

Key Stage 3
Resources

www.MyEducationalTests.co.uk